MW00490188

Wisdom of the Desert Fathers and Mothers

WISDOM OF THE DESERT FATHERS AND MOTHERS

Ancient Advice for the Modern World

Fr. Philip Bochanski

TAN Books
Gastonia, North Carolina

Cover design by Caroline Green

Cover image: 3D render of a desert scene by Kjpargeter / Shutterstock.

Library of Congress Control Number: 2019957435

ISBN: 978-1-5051-1415-7

Published in the United States by
TAN Books
PO Box 269
Gastonia, NC 28053
www.TANBooks.com

Printed and bound in the United States of America

Contents

PART ONE

Alone With God Alone

CHAPTER ONE

Why the Desert?

In the year 385, a twenty-five-year-old monk from Bethlehem felt called to gain a deeper understanding of his vocation, the life that God had called him to live. He and a friend, a fellow monk, traveled three hundred miles to the deserts of Lower Egypt, south of the great port city of Alexandria, to visit the monks living there, whose reputations had spread throughout the Mediterranean world. He went, he said, "If not for the sake of imitating them, then at least for the sake of becoming acquainted with them."[1] He had been thinking and praying, reading and studying about his vocation, and he needed to see in person how it was done.

Our traveler made a new friend there, an old man named Archebius, who had been a monk for over thirty-seven years in the desert and was now bishop of the city of Panephysis. Archebius said that he had been taken from

---

[1]   St. John Cassian, *The Conferences*, trans. Boniface Ramsey, Ancient Christian Writers Series, no. 57 (New York: Newman, 1997), XI.1.

his desert solitude because he had been unworthy of that vocation and had not made enough progress in all those years. When Archebius heard what his visitors were seeking, he offered to help them.

"Come," he said, "and visit for a while with the elders whose old age and holiness, in bodies now bent over, shines so brightly in their faces that the mere sight of them is able to teach a great deal to those who gaze upon them. From them you shall learn, not so much by words as by the example of a holy life, what I regret that I have let slip and am unable to teach, because I have already lost it."[2]

The young monk, whom we know now as St. John Cassian, spent the better part of fifteen years sitting at the feet of the monks in the Egyptian desert, learning from them the deep secrets of making a total renunciation of self and a complete commitment to purity of heart. Some twenty years later, at the request of his bishop in Marseilles, where Cassian himself had built a monastery, he wrote of his experiences in the desert. He insisted that he was no better than Bishop Archebius to do justice to what he saw there, much less to imitate it. Nevertheless, he related the lessons that he had learned so that others could benefit from them as well.

The aim of this book is the same that inspired Cassian: to share the life and the teachings of the great saints of the desert so that modern readers may draw inspiration and courage from their example and recommit themselves to the task of conversion and spiritual growth. To understand the monks of the ancient desert, it is necessary to

---

[2]   Ibid., XI.2.2.

rediscover both the world that they left behind and the new home that they encountered in the wilderness, alone with God alone.

Throughout the history of salvation, as recorded in the Sacred Scripture of both testaments, the desert frequently appears as a place to encounter God's presence and God's chosen locale for renewing his people and calling them to conversion and transformation. Above all, the story of the Exodus, when God rescued his people from slavery in Egypt and led them for forty years through the desert to the homeland he had prepared for them, shaped the life of the Jewish people and is imprinted deeply on the Christian consciousness as well. The desert of the Exodus was not only a place through which to journey but was the site of quite memorable miracles of God's protection and providence: manna from heaven, water from the rock, and protection from countless enemies.

At the end of their journey, encamped by the River Jordan, Moses urged the people to recall the things that the Lord had done for them. "You shall remember," he said, "all the way which the LORD your God has led you these forty years in the wilderness, that he might humble you, testing you to know what was in your heart, whether you would keep his commandments, or not. And he humbled you and let you hunger and fed you with manna . . . that he might make you know that man does not live by bread alone, but that man lives by everything that proceeds out of the mouth of the LORD" (Dt 8:2–3). Moses urged them never to forget the lessons God taught them in the desert, even by means of the suffering he permitted to befall them. "Know then in your heart," he told them, "that, as a man disciplines his son, the LORD your God disciplines you. So you shall keep the commandments of the LORD your God, by walking in his ways and by fearing him" (Dt 8:5–6).

Of course, we know from the history of salvation that time and again the people of God did forget his commandments. God sent the prophets to call his people back to him, and there, too, the desert became a place of transformation, a place of renewal. Speaking through the prophet Hosea, for example, God tells the people that he will call them back to the desert, where he will encounter them again as in the days of the Exodus and remind them of his love. Speaking of Israel as his bride, he tells Hosea, "I will allure her, and bring her into the wilderness, and speak tenderly to her. . . . And there she shall answer as in the days of her youth, as at the time when she came out of the land of Egypt" (Hos 2:14–15). Then speaking to Israel, he says, "And I will betroth you to me for ever; I will betroth you to me in righteousness and in justice, in steadfast love, and in mercy. I will betroth you to me in faithfulness; and you shall know the Lord" (Hos 2:19–20).

When they had been unfaithful, God drew his people back to the place where he had first met them. He drew them back to the wilderness, away from the busyness of the city and the burdens of daily life, to a quiet place where they could be renewed in his love and transformed by their time with him.

In the fullness of time, John the Baptist also appeared in the desert, calling the people to repentance, to make room in their hearts for the coming Messiah. Mark tells us, "John the baptizer appeared in the wilderness, preaching a baptism of repentance for the forgiveness of sins. And there went out to him all the country of Judea, and all the people of Jerusalem; and they were baptized by him in the river Jordan, confessing their sins" (Mk 1:4–5).

Jesus, too, went down to be baptized by John, and as soon as he came up from the water and was filled with the Holy Spirit, the Gospels all relate that he was moved by the Holy Spirit to go out himself into the desert. There he dwelt for forty days and forty nights (a symbolic number which appears in Scripture to signify a period of transformation) to be tested by the temptations of the devil. In the desert, he accepted a share in our own experience of temptation, and he returned from that desert experience filled with power and ready to begin his public ministry.

Clearly, the scriptural deserts were settings for transformative encounters with God. But what did it hold for those who fled there more than three hundred years after the time of Christ, some seventeen centuries after the Exodus?

The first half of the fourth century AD was a sort of "golden age" of desert monasticism. The great St. Anthony went deep into the desert, to his "Inner Mountain," around 313, and St. Pachomius founded the first large monastery at Tabennesi in 320. The famous monastery of Sketis was founded in 330, and the location known as the Cells in 338. In the cities, meanwhile, the Church was recovering from a long period of persecutions: under the emperors

Decius and Valens between 250 and 257, and under Dio-
cletian from 302 to 305.

Some of the first to enter the desert had fled there in
times of persecution. For example, St. Jerome related the
story of Paul of Thebes, better known as St. Paul the First
Hermit. Paul's parents died when he was just a child, and
Paul was left in the care of his sister and her husband.
Because women could not inherit property, Paul received
all of his parents' property, and when Paul was old enough
to take possession of it, his brother-in-law came up with
a scheme to take it for himself. Hearing that his brother-
in-law was ready to betray him to the civil authorities as
a Christian, Paul ran away and took refuge in the desert.
Finding that he was safe there, he also felt God calling
him to stay and lead a life of seclusion, to leave the world
and his inheritance behind and to dwell there in peace and
prayer. St. Jerome says that "what had been his necessity
became his free choice. . . . In this beloved habitation,
offered to him as it were by God himself, he lived his life
through in prayer and solitude. . . . For 113 years, Paul
lived a life of heaven upon earth."[3]

Following the Edict of Milan, by which Emperor Constantine gave official status to Christianity throughout the
empire in 313, persecutions had mostly ceased. At this
time, people began to turn to the desert not to escape persecution but in order to seek the kind of heroic challenge
and sacrifice that the martyrs of their parents' generation

---

[3]   St. Jerome, *Life of Saint Paul the First Hermit*, in *Early
Christian Lives*, trans. Carolinne White (London: Penguin,
1998).

had made. Many of them were from the capital city of Alexandria where, a generation earlier, a popular preacher named Origen had spoken about ways to live a life of heroic holiness. Origen's own father had been a martyr, and Origen wondered how in his day they would be able to distinguish those who were really ready to make the ultimate sacrifice for the Lord. Origen says, "If we truly judge the matter . . . we will see that we are not now faithful. But when noble martyrdom arose, then there were faithful [Christians]. . . . Then, the faithful were few but truly faithful, who traveled a way narrow and hard, which leads to life."[4]

The question for people in the generation after martyrdom was how to show heroic faithfulness to the Lord in a relatively peaceful, easy situation. They came to understand that there was another kind of battle to be fought, every bit as serious as the battle against the persecutor and, in many ways, more dangerous and harder to fight: the battle against the self.

In its Pastoral Constitution on the Church in the Modern World, *Gaudium et spes*, the Second Vatican Council speaks about this interior battle: "The whole of man's history has been the story of dour combat with the powers of evil, stretching, so our Lord tells us, from the very dawn of history until the last day. Finding himself in the midst of the battlefield, a person has to struggle to do what is right, and it is at great cost to himself and aided by God's grace that he succeeds in achieving his own inner integrity.[5] The

---

4   Origen, *Homilies on Jeremiah*, IV.iii.2.

5   Second Vatican Council, *Gaudium et spes*, 37.2.

Catechism of the Catholic Church explains, "The way of perfection passes by way of the Cross. There is no holiness without renunciation and spiritual battle. Spiritual progress entails the ascesis and mortification that gradually lead to living in the peace and joy of the Beatitudes."[6]

So, to respond to the call to radical holiness is to do battle against the self and against our desires. Origen explained that the whole of our life on earth involves a battle against temptations.[7] We will always experience hunger, because our bodies need food; we will have to deal with basic desires for bodily pleasure, because we have our bodies always with us. The basic needs that we feel are not evil in themselves, but they become bad for us when they are out of proportion or directed towards the wrong object. The battle against the self means bringing the body under the control of the soul and reminding the body that not every desire need be instantly gratified. Such a process of conversion and training of the self is by its nature life-long.

The *Catechism* explains that "feelings or passions are emotions or movements of the sensitive appetite that incline us to act or not to act in regard to something felt or imagined to be good or evil. The passions are natural components of the human psyche; they form the passageway and ensure the connection between the life of the senses and the life of the mind. . . . In themselves, passions are neither good nor evil. They are morally qualified to

---

6   *Catechism of the Catholic Church*, no. 2015.

7   Cf. Origen, *On Prayer*, XXIX.1.

the extent that they effectively engage reason and will."[8]
A person is responsible for maintaining vigilance over
the desires of mind, heart, and body and only choosing
to entertain and act on those desires which lead to what
is truly good. This was the daily work of those who went
out into the desert, to acquire not just mastery over themselves but experience and wisdom that they were able to
share with others.

St. John Cassian says, "It is no external adversary that
we must fear. The foe is within us, and every day we wage
an inner war. Once it has been conquered, everything that
is outside will be weakened, and all things will be sub-
dued and subjected to the soldier of Christ. We shall not
have an adversary outside of us to be afraid of, if what is
within us has been overcome and yielded to the spirit."[9]

Many people also went out to the desert not only to do
battle with the self but to seek opportunities for repentance
and for doing penance for past sins. By offering sufferings up to God, by going without the things that they had
become accustomed to, especially if their lives had been
particularly comfortable or luxurious by the standards
of their times, they hoped to be able to lead a life more
detached, more focused on God's will, and more responsive to his Word. Origen compared this life of conversion
and repentance to the work of a goldsmith. If a person
wants to make a vessel out of gold, he explained, "he has

---

[8]   *Catechism*, nos. 1763–64, 1767.

[9]   St. John Cassian, *The Institutes*, trans. Boniface Ramsey,
        Ancient Christian Writers series, no. 58 (New York: Newman,
        2000), V.xxi.1.

to bring it often to the fire, he has to strike it often with a hammer, he burnishes it often, so that it becomes more purified, and brought to the shape and the beauty intended by the artisan."[10] The monks of the desert went out to the wilderness to be reshaped according to the image and likeness of God in which they had been created, and which had been distorted or blurred by sin and selfishness.

---

[10]   Origen, *Homilies on Numbers*, XXVII.2.

CHAPTER TWO

The Development of Monasticism

To understand the daily life of the men and women who went to find God in the desert, it is necessary to begin with some vocabulary. The last chapter discussed the spiritual and physical battle that they underwent, which is most often referred to in Greek as *askēsis*—that is, "exercise" or "training." It comes into English as "ascesis," and its adjective form "ascetical," and refers to intentional sacrifices like taking less than the usual amount of food or sleep, or taking on voluntary penances and works of service. Often, those who were living an ascetical life were referred to as *athlētēs*, which has the same meaning as its English translation, "athletes." In Greek, it most often refers to the particular type of athlete we call a wrestler, someone who gains mastery over someone by an intense struggle and the use of his hands. The monks learned to master their passions and temptations through hand-to-hand combat, so to speak, by facing them and keeping them in check, often with the help of a one-on-one relationship with a spiritual father or spiritual mother.

In addition to these Greek terms, the Latin word used most often of the desert is *mortificatio*, the source of the English *mortification*. The word is derived from two Latin words: *mors*, which means "death," and *facere*, which means "to make." Mortification signifies putting to death the desires of the heart, a voluntary sacrifice that one makes in imitation of Christ and his sacrifice of himself on the cross. It is not suffering for its own sake, however. Rather, when a person puts his sins to death by being crucified daily with Christ, he is granted an opportunity to share likewise in a daily resurrection, a return to a new way of living.

The mortification of the desert took many forms. First, the flight from the world itself brought many sacrifices, especially for those who lived comfortably in the cities. One famous monk, St. Arsenius, had been a tutor to the children of the emperor. He lived in the palace and had rich food every day, fine clothes to wear, all kinds of entertainment—a very easy and luxurious existence. But while in the palace one day, Arsenius asked the Lord, "Lead me in the way of salvation," and he heard a voice call out to him, "Arsenius, flee from here. Flee from the company of human beings and you will be saved."[1] So he got up at once and went into the desert, becoming the most ascetical of the monks where he was dwelling. He learned from this experience the truth that a monk named Abba Pinufius once told a new arrival to the desert, "We must enter

---

[1]   Cf. *The Sayings of the Desert Fathers: The Alphabetical Collection* ("Alphabetikon"), Arsenius, trans. Benedicta Ward (Kalamazoo, Mich.: Cistercian Publications, 1975), 1, 4.

the Kingdom of God through many tribulations. . . . You should know that on this day," by joining the monastery, "you have died to the world and to its deeds and desires."[2]

Still, the monks were urged not to consider their sacrifices as something about which to boast. St. Anthony of Egypt, for example, warned his monks not to consider their flight from the world as any great thing, because the world, compared to heaven, is so small. "Children," he said, "let us not weary or think that we are doing something great. . . . Neither let us look back upon the world and think that we have renounced great things. For even the whole world is a very trifling thing, compared with all of heaven. . . . What we leave behind is practically nothing."[3]

One more term deserves attention, though it has come up many times already: *monk*, and its related term, *monastery*. Both originate in the Greek word *monos*, which means "alone, single, one." It is reflected in the prefix of many words in English: *monotone, monopoly, monogamy*, and the like. From *monos* comes *monachós*, "a monk" (literally, "a person who lives alone"), as well as *monē*, "a monastery," where monks lived a life of solitude and prayer.

Although modern readers often think of monasteries as large residences where many monks live together, it was not always so. St. John Climacus (his surname means "of

---

2   Cassian, *Institutes* IV.34, 38.

3   St. Athanasius, *The Life of Saint Antony*, trans. Robert T. Meyer, Ancient Christian Writers series, no. 10 (New York: Newman, 1950), 17.

the Ladder," because he was the author of *The Ladder of Divine Ascent*) described three ways to live the monastic vocation. Some monks lived completely by themselves, what Climacus calls "the retirement and solitude of a spiritual athlete." Some chose "living in stillness with one or two others," while others opted for "settling patiently in a community."[4]

The monks who chose solitude by themselves or with a few others lived in what came to be known as a *cell*, a small dwelling that could take the form of a cave, a hut, or even a mausoleum. At first, these cells were located not in the desert but on the outskirts of the cities. The cells were places where people could withdraw from the busyness of the city, and that provided shelter from the elements and enough peace and quiet to live a dedicated life of prayer. Because the cells were at first located along roads in and out of the city, people passing by would notice the monks living there and sometimes stay and ask their advice and their prayers. Rufinus, who wrote a *History of the Monks in Egypt*, notes that in his time, "There is no town or village in Egypt . . . which is not surrounded by hermitages as if by walls. And the people depend on the prayers of these monks as if on God himself."[5] The word that we

---

4   St. John Climacus, *The Ladder of Divine Ascent*, trans. Colm Luibheid and Norman Russell, Classics of Western Spirituality series (Mahwah, N.J.: Paulist, 1982), I.26.

5   Rufinus, *History of the Monks in Egypt*, Prologue, in *The Lives of the Desert Fathers: The* Historia Monachorum in Aegypto, trans. Norman Russell (Kalamazoo, Mich.: Cistercian Publications, 1981), 10.

translate as "hermitage" is *erēmos*, literally, "a place for being alone."

Eventually, monks who desired a more secluded life went farther from the city and into the desert itself. St. Paphnutius, in *The Life of Saint Onuphrius*, tells a dramatic story of one of them. Wandering one day in the deserts of Upper Egypt, Paphnutius saw a man in the distance, with long hair growing all over his body, whose appearance resembled more a wild animal than a civilized man. Paphnutius climbed the side of a mountain to get away from this stranger, but the desert dweller followed him. "He saw me," Paphnutius relates, "and called, 'Come down to me, holy man. I too am a man of the desert like yourself. I live in this desert on account of my sins.' . . . 'My name is Onuphrius and for sixty years I have lived in this desert. I walk in the mountains like a wild beast and I've never seen anyone I recognize.'"[6]

Paphnutius was amazed that anyone could live like this, not just in a cell, on the outskirts of the city, but completely isolated for sixty years, not laying eyes on any other human being in all that time. Onuphrius related, however, that this radical sacrifice was accepted and rewarded by God with miraculous gifts of providence reminiscent of the stories of the Exodus. "When God saw that I patiently endured in the good fight of fasting," he told Paphnutius, "and that I devoted myself completely to ascetic practices, he had his holy angels serve me with my daily food. . . . The palm tree here produced for me twelve bunches of dates each

---

[6]   Paphnutius, *The Life of St. Onuphrius*, trans. Tim Vivian (Kalamazoo, Mich.: Cistercian Publications, 1993), 10.

year, and I would eat one bunch every month. And he also made the plants that grow in the desert sweet as honey in my mouth."[7] Then he related the most wonderful miracle of all. He was hundreds of miles from any church where he could receive the sacraments, but, he said, an angel of God came to give him Holy Communion every weekend on Saturday and Sunday. Onuphrius reported that all of the hermits who lived in the desert received the same miracle: that if they were too far away to receive Holy Communion from a human being, that angels would come to bring them the Eucharist.[8]

Other hermits distanced themselves from the city vertically, rather than horizontally. The most famous of these was St. Simeon the Stylite, whose name comes from the Greek word for a pillar. After living in a monastery for three years, Simeon built a large pole on the outskirts of town, climbed to the top, and lived there for four years, completely exposed to snow, rain, and the heat of the sun. People sought him out and asked for his advice and prayers, and so he gradually relocated to higher and higher pillars—a six-foot pole just wide enough for him to stand, where he lived for seven years; and then a forty-five-foot pole on which he stood for fifteen years. This solitude and ascesis gave him the opportunity for an intense life of prayer, which God rewarded by granting St. Simeon the power to perform miraculous healings for many people.

As more monks moved to the desert, they found not only safety in numbers but solace in being able to see one

---

7   Ibid., 16.
8   Cf. ibid., 17.

another occasionally for counsel and prayer. The next development in the desert life was the establishment of *lauras*, from the Greek word for "alleys." In a *laura*, a number of cells would be built in relative proximity to each other—far enough apart to ensure solitude but close enough to permit occasional visits. For example, St. Anthony, after moving from the city to the desert, lived in complete isolation for twenty years. When he finally emerged from his solitude, a large crowd gathered to see him and to ask about his experience. He encouraged them to stay and follow the way of life he had adopted, and so a *laura* of several dozen cells became one of the first instances of an organized common life in the desert.

The desert way of life quickly attracted greater numbers of people to the desert, and the *lauras* of small cells gave way to larger residences, more in line with what the modern reader thinks of as a monastery. Eventually the monasteries were as large as small cities, growing up in various places in the Egyptian deserts. As they grew and became better organized, those who founded and led them wrote rules to guide the common life of the residents.

Among the first to compose a rule for desert monks was St. Pachomius, who first lived in a *laura* like St. Anthony's. Naturally, the foundation of the monastic life was their shared commitment to ascesis. "We always spend half the night, and often even from evening to morning, in vigils and the recitation of the Word of God," Pachomius wrote. The monks also carried out "manual work with threads, hairs or palm-fibers," making ropes, mats, and baskets, "lest we be overcome by sleep."[9] They ate very sparingly, never tasting meat or drinking wine. They fasted all day until late afternoon or evening, only eating once a day during the summer, and only every second or third day during the winter. They prayed sixty prayers together, mostly psalms, during the day, and fifty prayers together during the night.

After many years leading this small community in the *laura*, Pachomius had a vision of the Lord, who told him, "Pachomius, struggle, dwell in this place and build a monastery, for many will come to you to become monks with you, and they will profit their souls."[10] As his reputation spread throughout Egypt, Pachomius did receive many visitors, sometimes thirty or forty at a time, who wished to learn from his example and to dwell with him. They found that life together provided its own challenges and benefits, as later writers about monasticism would relate. Cassian, for example, notes that "when contact with other human beings ceases, along with the discipline that that provides, the vices grow wilder in us if they have not previously been purged."[11] Likewise, Climacus sees in the common life the cure for selfishness and a grouchy disposition. "Take a hard stone," he says, "with sharp corners. Knock

---

[9]   *The Life of Saint Pachomius*, in *Pachomian Koinonia: The Lives, Rules and Other Writings of Saint Pachomius and His Disciples*, in three volumes, trans. Armand Veilleux (Kalamazoo, Mich.: Cistercian Publications, 1980, 1982, 1989), 10.

[10]   Ibid., 17.

[11]   Cassian, *Institutes*, VIII.xviii.

it and rub it against other stones until its sharpness and hardness are crushed by the knocking and rubbing and, at last, it is made round. So, too, take a soul that is rough and abrupt, put it into the community and company of tough, short-tempered men."[12] This contact, Climacus says, will either wear off the rough edges on the grouchy monk's personality and make him humble and patient or he will leave the monastery altogether.

So the idea of a monastery as a place to seek solitude and to grow in holiness through a common way of life gave rise to the *cenobium*. This Greek word comes from two other: *koinos*, which means "together," and *bios*, which means "life." So the cenobium, a place for living together, was a building surrounded with a wall to protect it from barbarians and thieves who would be passing by. It comprised a number of dormitories and common areas, with a church at the center of the complex, and a dining hall. Such a monastery could hold, in some cases, up to 1,200 or 1,600 monks at a time,[13] quite a change from a *laura*, which was usually organized with one spiritual father and five or six disciples.

Monasteries like that built by Pachomius were wonders of organization. House masters were assigned for each household of monks, who were given tasks to do to support the community. Some monks made baskets, some wove mats, some were tailors, some fixed the carriages, some made shoes, some made clothing. They lived in

---

[12]   Climacus, *The Ladder*, VIII.

[13]   Cf. St. Jerome, preface to *The Rules of Saint Pachomius*, in *Pachomian Koinonia*, op. cit., 2.

dormitories organized by their crafts so that their supplies could be given out efficiently and they could be trained for their work together as "one family," as St. Jerome records.

Jerome says that the superiors of all Pachomius's monasteries had one head, living at the monastery of Phbow, who organized the monks and gathered them all together on major feast days. He writes that "in the days of the Passover," meaning for the Easter feast, "all assemble around him except those who are needed in their own monasteries, so that nearly 50,000 men celebrate together the feast of the Lord's Passion."[14]

We can marvel at the different ways that life in the desert adapted to the people who were there, whether they lived as hermits in complete solitude, small communities in a *laura*, or large groups in a cenobium. Although the monks went out for many different reasons, and lived in rather different ways from one another, the goal that they had was in many ways the same. All of their daily habits, all of their many rules, were heading towards one common purpose: purity of heart.

---

[14]   Ibid., 7.

CHAPTER THREE

Daily Life in the Desert

The first step into the monastery began with a knock at the door. *The Rules of Saint Pachomius* say that when someone came to the door of the monastery, he was not to be admitted right away. Instead, the monk who was assigned to the door, known as the porter, was to tell him that he had to stay outside for a few days. The porter would then speak to him through a window constructed next to the door and teach him "the Lord's Prayer and as many psalms as he can learn."[1]

Next, the porter was to investigate who this person was. The candidate was supposed to make himself known, to explain why he had come to the monastery. Had he done something wrong? Was he troubled by fear? Had he run away from some bad situation at home? Was he under someone's authority? Had he been a soldier? Was he a runaway slave? The porter, through gentle conversation, had to determine whether this person was ready for the

---

[1]   *The Rules of Saint Pachomius*, Precepts, in *Pachomian Koinonia*, op. cit., 49.

monastic life. Was he able to renounce his parents and his family and his home? Could he leave his possessions behind? Could he really give up his old life? The porter had to do what he could to find out the reasons why the candidate wanted to renounce the world.

The *Catechism* explains that "Jesus enjoins his disciples to prefer him to everything and everyone, and bids them to 'renounce all [they] have' for his sake and that of the Gospel. The precept of detachment from riches is obligatory for entrance into the kingdom of heaven."[2] The precept to be detached, and not to let our possessions possess us, belongs to every disciple. But the Lord calls some of his disciples to accept this precept, this evangelical counsel, in a radical way, so as to give themselves to him more completely and to be an example, encouragement, and even a challenge to the rest of the Church. By the radical example of a few, all may understand their own vocation and their own need for detachment. The *Catechism*, quoting *Lumen gentium*, says that "all Christ's faithful are to 'direct their affections rightly, less they be hindered in their pursuit of perfect charity by the use of worldly things and by an adherence to riches that is contrary to the spirit of evangelical poverty'"—that is, detachment in imitation of Christ himself.[3]

The monk who said that he was ready to be detached, who came to the monastery wanting to leave the world behind, would have to persevere at the door of the monastery for several days or even, in some cases, for several

---

2   *Catechism*, no. 2544, quoting Mk 8:35.

3   Ibid., no. 2545, quoting *Lumen gentium* 42.3.

weeks. If the porter, who was especially chosen for this job because of his experience and his kindness, saw that he was ready and was willing to persevere, then he would bring him in and start to teach him the rest of what it meant to be a monk: what he had to do and whom he had to serve.

If he was willing to accept instruction, then he would be admitted further into the monastery and be allowed to join the brothers. The first step after he was brought inside was to leave the world behind in terms of outward things. This included anything that he had brought with him; he was not allowed to bring any possessions into the monastery, nor any money. All those things he would have to give away before he entered the door. And then even his clothes would be taken away from him. He would be stripped of his secular clothes and given instead a monastic habit; all the monks in the monastery were dressed exactly alike. He handed over his clothes to the porter and was given new clothes to wear without being able to choose his size or the style that he preferred. The ancient monastic rules often advised that the monastery hold on to the monk's clothing for a period of several months, to make sure that he had the spirit and the strength to persevere. Once they knew that he would be able to endure, they would give away to the poor the clothes that he brought with him.

St. Jerome says that in these monasteries, the monks would have no possessions except a mat and two monastic habits, which consisted of a garment without sleeves, "a linen mantle, two hoods, a goat skin" to wear in inclement weather, "a linen belt, and finally shoes and a staff to go on journeys."[4] In addition, they would be given a second sleeveless garment, older and worn, to wear while working and sleeping.

The parts of the habit had a complex significance, sometimes practical, sometimes symbolic. For example, the monastic habit did not have long sleeves, because in Egyptian culture they could be interpreted as a sign of worldliness. They also could get in the way of the work that the monks had to do. The habit had a hood, which in Egypt was usually only worn by children. They wore it as a sign of humility, and that they were willing to make themselves small because they were just beginners in the life of holiness. Wearing the hood also provided a certain amount of privacy and freedom from distraction when the monks came together to pray.

Each dormitory had a house master who made sure that the habits and other necessities were distributed to each one equally.

No one was allowed to serve as house master unless he recognized that he also was under the authority of others; every monk had to learn to be obedient, to renounce his own will, and to see himself as the least important of all. This battle against pride, selfishness, and self-importance was a necessary first step in learning to be obedient and responsive to the will of God. To leave the monastery always required the permission of the abbot, for example, and the *Rule of Saint Pachomius* said that "no one shall go out into the fields, walk around in the monastery, or go

---

[4]   St. Jerome, preface to *The Rules of Saint Pachomius*, 4.

outside the monastery wall without requesting and receiving the house master's permission."[5]

Most important in terms of learning obedience was the relationship that was created between a young monk and a monk with more experience. As Cassian explains, "The young monks are taught never through a hurtful shame to hide any of the thoughts in their hearts that come from the evil one, but to reveal them to their *abba* as soon as they surface. Nor to judge them in accordance with their own discretion but as the *abba*'s examination discloses and makes clear."[6] This word *abba* comes from the Syriac language, and also appears in the biblical language Aramaic. It means "father" and is the root word of words like *abbey* and *abbot*, which refer to a monastic house and its head, respectively. The feminine cognate for *abba* is *amma,* which means "mother."

Abbas and *ammas*, fathers and mothers, were the older generation in the monastery, who learned from long experience the ways of serving God.[7] They would take younger monks and nuns under their guidance and discuss with them the things that were going on in their minds and in their hearts.

The relationship with the *abba* was the central relationship in the life of the monk, and has a parallel in what is

---

5   Ibid., 85.

6   Cassian, *Institutes*, IV.ix.

7   Sometimes an *abba* is called by the Greek term *gerōn*, which means "an old man." This was not used pejoratively but as a sign of respect for the wisdom that the *abba/geron* had acquired over long years in the monastery.

usually called "spiritual direction." It is a relationship still seen as very central to those who are serious about growing in holiness; as the *Catechism* explains, "The Holy Spirit gives to certain of the faithful the gifts of wisdom, faith, and discernment for the sake of this common good, which is prayer (this is called *spiritual direction*). Men and women so endowed are true servants of the living tradition of prayer."[8]

"The person wishing to advance toward perfection," the *Catechism* goes on, should, as St. John of the Cross suggests, "take care into whose hands he entrusts himself. For as the master is, so will the disciple be. And as the father is, so will be the son. . . . In addition to being learned and discrete," St. John continues, "a director should be experienced. Otherwise he will be incapable of leading . . . the souls whom God is calling, and he will not even understand them."[9]

Every *abba* had had an *abba* of his own at one point, of course. Each monk would go to see his *abba* at fixed times, sometimes every day. They were taught to always be honest with the *abba*, and to share frankly whatever thoughts were passing through their minds, whatever temptations were afflicting them, and whatever questions they had about their future. The ability to have an honest and free discussion about everything that was troubling them, without hiding anything out of shame or a desire to impress, and to follow the *abba's* advice rather than their

---

8   *Catechism,* 2690.
9   Ibid., quoting St. John of the Cross, *The Living Flame of Love,* 3.30.

own opinions or preferences, was essential for the long-term perseverance of the younger monks.

St. John Cassian says that the monks were taught to "follow those who we recognize have shaped their lives in a praiseworthy and upright manner as young men, and who have been instructed not in their own presumptions but in the traditions of their forebears."[10] He explains how easy it is for the devil to deceive a young and inexperienced monk who is trying to do things on his own, to hold him back through embarrassment and concern for his own image. Once the monk is able in humility to turn over his struggles to someone else, then he immediately receives the help he needs, and finds that his burden is lessened because he had been able to share it. "As soon as a wicked thought has been revealed, it loses its power," Cassian says, "and the loathsome serpent," the devil, "departs as a kind of laughing stock and object of dishonor. For his harmful counsels hold sway in us as long as they lie concealed in our heart."[11]

St. John Climacus echoes this advice. He says that the monks "should turn humbly and in confidence to the Fathers . . . and accept their counsel as though from God himself, even when that counsel goes against the grain, even when the advice comes from those who do not seem very spiritual. Even if those consulted are stupid," he concludes, "God invisibly speaks through them, and anyone

---

[10]   Cassian, *The Conferences*, II.xiii.2.

[11]   Ibid., II.x.3.

who faithfully submits to this norm will be filled with humility."[12]

In addition to spiritual counsel and constant prayer, life in the cenobium was organized for manual labor. As the *Rule of Saint Pachomius* says, "The house master and his assistant must plait 25 fathoms of palm leaves, so that the others may work after their example."[13] Such labor served several purposes. The monks made certain crafts—ropes, mats, and baskets of palm leaves, for example—so that they could trade them for supplies, food, textiles, and other necessities. More importantly, carrying out manual labor with the body allowed the monks to ward off distractions during prayers in the middle of the night, or during times of silence. Keeping their distractible bodies occupied gave them freedom to focus their minds and hearts more intently on prayer. They trained their bodies to work quietly so that their hearts could be in deeper communication with God.

A peculiar feature of the monastic life was the fact that, although most of the ancient world was illiterate, almost everyone in the monastery was able to read. The *Rule of Saint Pachomius* insisted that anyone who came to the monastery without this skill had to be taught it first. "If he is illiterate, he shall go at 6:00 am, at 9:00 am, and at noon to someone who can teach and has been appointed for him. He shall stand before him and learn very studiously with all gratitude. Even if he does not want to, he shall be compelled to read. There shall be no one in the

---

[12]   Climacus, *The Ladder*, XXVI.

[13]   *The Rules of Saint Pachomius*, Precepts and Laws, 1.3.

monastery whatever who does not learn to read and who does not memorize something of the Scripture."[14]

The monks spent large portions of the day and night in prayer, and most of their prayers came from the Sacred Scripture. To copy manuscripts by hand was very labor intensive, so the monks had to be able to read in order to use what scrolls there were available and to memorize the Scriptures very quickly. They also had to be able to share the work of reading the Scriptures in the gathering for prayer; for a monk to skip his turn doing a job that was common to all the monks would have been a violation of the rule and of the virtues of humility and obedience. Thus, every monk learned to read.

The monks prayed in common frequently, and were expected to observe the set times for daily prayer wherever they were. "Whether he is on a boat," Pachomius says, "in the monastery, in the fields, or on a journey, or fulfilling any service whatever," he was supposed to keep in mind his schedule and say prayers with his fellow monks wherever he happened to be.[15] When all the monks gathered for common prayers, they divided up the prayers among them so that everyone gave unbroken praise to God. When they returned to their cells from praying together, they spent some more time before they went to bed praying, each of them alone in their cells giving praise and worship to God and following upon the meditation that they had heard in the gathering place, bringing it back to mind and keeping it in their hearts.

---

[14]   Ibid., Precepts, 139–40.

[15]   Ibid., 141–42.

Rufinus, talking about the monks in Egypt, described them as "loyal sons watching for their father, or like an army expecting its emperor, or a like a sober household looking forward to the arrival of its master and liberator."[16] He saw there "no anxiety for food and clothing," no worry about material things, but "only the expectation of the coming of Christ."[17] The monks expressed this anticipation especially in prayers through the night, and in strict fasting. Keeping themselves prepared for the coming of Christ meant that even basic bodily necessities like sleep or food would be sacrificed willingly. But Cassian insists that "these observances do not exist for themselves." Rather, the monks "carry out the things that are secondary—namely fasts, vigils, the solitary life and meditation on Scriptures—for the sake of the principal goal, which is purity of heart and love."[18] "We should not believe," he says, "that mere fasting from visible food can suffice for our perfection of heart and purity of body, if a fasting of the soul has not also been joined to it. . . . For fleshly toil joined to a contrite spirit will produce a sacrifice most acceptable to God and a worthy dwelling for holiness in the pure and clean depths of our heart."[19] "For the sake of purity of heart, everything is to be done and desired," he says. "For its sake solitude is to be pursued; for its sake we

---

16   *History of the Monks in Egypt*, Prologue, 7.
17   Ibid.
18   *Conferences*, I.vii.2.
19   *Institutes*, V.xxi.1–4.

know that we must undertake fasts, vigils, labors, bodily deprivations, readings, and other virtuous things."[20]

At the heart of the Beatitudes, those rules for living that the Lord Jesus gives at the beginning of the Sermon on the Mount, we find the admonition, "Blessed are the pure in heart, for they shall see God" (Mt 5:8). Here is the underlying purpose of all the ascetical works, all the prayers and all the rules that the monks followed in the desert. By putting away the things of the world, and removing any obstacles to an undivided heart, they believed that they would see God more clearly in this life, and enjoy the vision of God forever in heaven. Although few people in the modern world can live the radical asceticism of the desert, everyone can pursue that same goal: a greater purity of heart that leads to a clearer vision of God and his plan for our lives.

---

[20] *Conferences,* I.vii.1.

PART TWO

St. Anthony the Great

CHAPTER FOUR

The Life of Anthony

O ur subject for the next few chapters is St. Anthony of Egypt, also known as St. Anthony the Great. There are many reasons that he deserved that title, and we can gauge his importance by the impact he had on another great figure in the history of the Church: St. Augustine.

After a tumultuous youth, Augustine found himself in the imperial city of Milan in the year 386, the last of his circle of friends who had not converted to Christianity. In his spiritual autobiography, known as *The Confessions,* he relates that, "on a certain day, Ponticianus, a fellow countryman of ours from Africa who held high office in the emperor's court," came to see him. "What he wanted with us," Augustine says, "I do not know, but we sat down to talk together. . . . A conversation followed in which he spoke of Anthony, the Egyptian monk, whose name was in high repute among [God's] servants, although up to that time, not familiar to me."[1]

Anthony of Egypt had died around the time Augustine

---

[1]   St. Augustine, *Confessions*, VIII.14.

was born, and Ponticianus had been reading the biography of Anthony that was written by St. Athanasius, the bishop of Alexandria, which had spread like wildfire throughout the ancient world. When Ponticianus learned that Augustine had never heard of Anthony, he started to fill him in on the story. "When he learned this," Augustine says, "he lingered on the topic, giving us an account of this eminent man and marveling at our ignorance. We, in turn, were amazed to hear of your wonderful works so fully manifested in recent times . . . occurring in the true faith and the Catholic Church. We all wondered—we, that these things were so great, and Ponticianus, that we had never heard of them. He went on with his story and we listened intently and in silence."[2]

Augustine then relates the story that Ponticianus told him, about how lots of people, hearing Anthony's story, had been inspired themselves to follow his example; how two friends coming upon the book in a certain house had left their whole life behind; and how Ponticianus himself, along with a friend, had decided to change his life: to resign his position in the emperor's court, to give away all his possessions, and to live a life dedicated to serving God and the Church.[3]

Augustine was troubled hearing this, trying to decide what to do. As he relates in *The Confessions*, addressing the Lord and recalling that moment:

---

[2]   Ibid.

[3]   Cf. ibid., 15.

While he was speaking, thou, O Lord, turned me
toward myself, taking me from behind my back
where I had put myself while unwilling to exercise
self-scrutiny. And now you set me face to face with
myself, that I might see how ugly I was. . . . I had
known it, but acted as though I knew it not. I winked
at it and forgot it. And here I was, still postponing
the abandonment of this world's happiness to devote
myself to the search. . . . Now the day had arrived
in which I was laid bare to myself. . . . Thus was I
inwardly confused, and mightily confounded with
a horrible shame, while Ponticianus went ahead
speaking such things.[4]

When Augustine heard about St. Anthony and how he
had lived, and how his example had inspired so many
other people to change their lives, he came to a moment
of crisis. It was clear to him that he also had to respond
to the invitation to follow Christ wholeheartedly. This
moment was the beginning of Augustine's struggle with
himself that eventually led to his conversion, and the road
that would make him a saint. This three-times-removed
encounter with St. Anthony enabled Augustine to trust
God completely. Let us hope that our own encounter with
Anthony can bear such fruit.

Anthony of Egypt was born about forty miles south
of Alexandria, along the Nile River. This meant that he
was close enough to visit Alexandria, the capital of Egypt
in those days, and to be influenced by the preaching of

---

[4]   Ibid., 16-18.

people like Origen, one of the most influential preachers of the third century. The place where Anthony was born was largely an agricultural community, and Athanasius, his biographer, tells us that his parents were well-to-do and had a fairly large farm.

Anthony was born around the year 251. In his youth, although he had the opportunity to receive formal schooling, he did not enjoy it or take it seriously. He went to church frequently with his parents, however, and always paid close attention to the Scriptures that were read there. Athanasius tells us that Anthony was satisfied with a simple life at home, with simple food, and never dressed ostentatiously. He had one sister, and his parents' death when Anthony was about eighteen or twenty years old left him responsible for her care, as well as for the family estate and the farm.

About six months after his parents' death, Anthony received his vocation. Curiously, he encountered it by showing up late for Mass. As he walked into church that day, the Gospel was being read: Matthew, chapter 19, the story of Jesus and the "rich young man." In response to the youth's earnest desire to seek perfection beyond just keeping the commandments, "Jesus said to him, 'If you would be perfect, go, sell what you possess and give to the poor, and you will have treasure in heaven; and come, follow me' " (Mt 19:21). Anthony walked in while this last sentence was being read, and felt in his heart that it was directed just at him; that in that moment, the Lord was revealing his plan for Anthony's life. Upon returning home, he decided to give almost all of his property away, keeping just the house and enough money for him and his sister to live on. Over the next few months, they survived as best they could on that simple amount.

A few months later, Anthony had a similar experience, again in church at the time of the Gospel. This time, the reading was from the sixth chapter of Matthew's Gospel, where Jesus says, in the Sermon on the Mount, "Do not be anxious about tomorrow, for tomorrow will be anxious for itself" (Mt 6:34). Anthony felt that the Lord was reassuring him with a second word about his vocation. He went home, talked things over with his sister, and found a place for her among a community of widows who would care for her. Then he sold the house, gave all the money that he had to the poor, and decided to live in complete dedication to God.

Thus, around the year 275, Anthony began an ascetical life, a process of solitary training in holiness. He did this first on the outskirts of the village where he was born. There were holy men living there, in the kind of cells or hermitages we have already mentioned. Although Anthony is often called the "Father of Monks," it is clear that he was not the first to follow God in a desire for holiness, and through the workings of divine providence, he was able to learn the ways of asceticism by spending time with these holy men. St. Athanasius describes Anthony "like a wise bee" going around from one hermit to another, like a bee flying from flower to flower, taking what is best from each one.[5]

Athanasius says, "If he heard of a zealous soul anywhere

---

[5]   St. Athanasius, *The Life of St. Antony*, 3.

. . . he left to search him out; nor did he return home before he had seen him, and only when he had received from him, as it were, provisions for his journey to virtue, did he go back. He made it his endeavor to learn for his own benefit just how each was superior to him in zeal and ascetic practice. . . . In one and all alike, he marked especially devotion to Christ and the love they had for one another."[6]

Athanasius points out that what Anthony was especially trying to learn was how these monks loved not only Christ but also each other. A monk means someone who lives alone, but Anthony noticed the charity that they had for each other as well as for the people that passed by on their way in and out of town, and those who came to seek them out, to ask for advice, prayers, and intercession for miraculous healings. This realization stayed with Anthony throughout his life. Although as a monk he would always seek solitude and a relationship with God alone, he kept his heart open to charity for his neighbor and sought to love Christ in the people who came to him.

After some time spent learning from these hermits near the village, Anthony, "having thus taken his fill, returned to his own place of asceticism. Then he assimilated what he had obtained from each, and devoted all his energies to realizing in himself the virtues of all."[7] He incorporated all the best things that he had found and tried to excel in each of them and to incorporate them into one holy life.

At this point, we encounter a theme that recurs often in the life of Anthony. Whenever he is making progress,

---

6   Ibid., 3–4.

7   Ibid., 4.

and things seem to be going well, the devil tries to put obstacles in his path. In these early days, Athanasius tells us that "the devil, the hater and envier of good, could not bear to see such resolution in a young man, but set about employing his customary tactics also against him."[8] First he is tempted to think about the things he has left behind, to consider his sister and wonder whether or not she was doing well. Of course, Anthony had already determined that: he had carefully chosen the community of widows where he had placed her and knew them to be trustworthy, so he was able quickly to put that thought out of his mind. Next came temptations of money, fame, and pleasure. Athanasius relates how, as Anthony walked along, he saw a bag of money lying by the road, or, on one occasion, a gold disk lying directly in front of him. On each occasion, Anthony made the sign of the cross, or spoke the name of Jesus, and the temptation disappeared in front of him in a puff of smoke.

The devil even appeared to him in the form of beautiful young women who tried to tempt him to impurity. Anthony was a youth in his early twenties at this time, but he stayed true to the commitment that he had made and offered himself as a complete sacrifice to the Lord. Resisting these temptations and turning wholeheartedly and courageously to prayer, he was so successful that, as St. Athanasius says, "the entire experience put the Enemy to shame."[9]

Anthony learned by these experiences always to be on

---

[8]   Ibid., 5.

[9]   Ibid.

his guard. He paid attention, Athanasius says, not to how long he had already been on the road to holiness but to how far he still needed to go. Each time he was tempted, Anthony redoubled his efforts at the ascetical life, undertaking vigils and fasting, denying his body the comforts that it wanted. Athanasius says that "Anthony did not grow careless and take too much for granted with himself," merely because he happened to conquer the devil this one time, and the devil certainly didn't give up just because he had not succeeded on this one occasion.[10] On the contrary, Anthony redoubled his efforts and kept an even closer watch, aware that, before long, the temptations would return.

After a few years living this life on the outskirts of the village, Anthony decided to take another step: to move farther out and become even more detached from the distractions of the world. He found a rather unlikely place for his next dwelling: a cemetery, where he took up residence in an old tomb for several years. During that time, he faced a severe confrontation with the demons, which would become another turning point in his life.

The demons appeared to him over the course of several days in various horrific forms. Some appeared as wild animals, others as fantastic monsters, that charge at him, roaring, clawing, and making all sorts of noises. In return, Anthony mocked the demons, with jibes like, "Here I am, Anthony. I am not cowed by your blows, and even though you should give me more, nothing shall separate me from

---

10   Ibid., 7.

the love of Christ."[11] The demons kept up their assault, moving from noisy roaring to physical assaults. They beat Anthony and jumped on him, attacking him over the course of three days. As a result, Anthony found himself worn out, exhausted, and unable to move.

At this point, he was visited by friends from the village, who found him in this weakened state and feared that he may be dead. They dragged him back to town and gathered the parish priest and the whole community in the church. They kept vigil over him late into the night, and eventually they all fell asleep. In the middle of the night, Anthony woke up, unsure of his surroundings. He roused his friend, who was sitting close by, and demanded to be taken back to his hermitage.

Once Anthony was resettled and his friend had left, the assaults of the demons resumed. Although too weak to move, Anthony remained as defiant as before. "If you had any power in you," he taunted them, "it would have been enough for just one of you to come; but the Lord has taken your strength away, and so you are trying, if possible to scare me out of my wits by your numbers. It is a sign of your helplessness. . . . If you can, and have received power against me, do not delay, but up and at me!"[12]

After about a day and a half more, suddenly a bright light appeared in Anthony's cell, emanating from the top corner of the room. The light spread throughout the whole area and frightened away the demons, and the pain in Anthony's body likewise disappeared. Looking up,

---

[11]   Ibid., 9.

[12]   Ibid.

Anthony saw a vision of the Lord Jesus in the center of the light, but his reaction may strike us as strange. "Where were you?" Anthony demanded of the Lord. "Why did you not appear at the beginning to stop my pains?"[13]

The Lord calmly responded, "Anthony, I was right here, but I waited to see you in action. And now, because you held out and did not surrender, I will ever be your helper and I will make you renowned everywhere."[14] Anthony learned through this difficult experience to trust in the Lord's presence and to rely on the Lord's strength and not his own. He also came to understand that sometimes God permits a trial, even a devastating one, for a deeper purpose, in order to teach an important lesson. Emerging from this trial, as Athanasius relates, "he was so strengthened that he felt his body more vigorous than before."[15]

The very next day, Anthony took another step along his path of holiness. He moved from the tomb where he had been living to what has come to be known as "The Outer Mountain," Mount Pispir, across the Nile from his birthplace, about thirty miles away. The year was 286, and Anthony was about thirty years old. At Mount Pispir, he found an old military fort, abandoned by the Egyptian army but still in fairly decent condition. Anthony decided to live there in solitude and began by clearing out the serpents and other creeping things, then planting a little garden for himself.

Travelers had made a route for themselves along a

---

13   Ibid., 10.
14   Ibid.
15   Ibid.

road nearby, and for a while, they brought him food and some companionship on a regular basis, about twice a year. His friends came to see him and tried to prevail on Anthony to come back closer to the village so that they could visit him more easily. Instead, craving even deeper solitude, Anthony shut the door of the fort and sealed it from the inside. He remained shut in for the next twenty years. During this time, the traveling merchants he had befriended brought him bread twice a year, handing it through a small window. Otherwise, Anthony saw and conversed with no one, until his friends came, in 306, to break down the door.

Anthony was now fifty-six years old, an old man for his time, and his friends expected to see a broken, weary, emaciated man emerge from the fort. Instead, he looked healthier and younger than ever. As St. Athanasius put it, "He came forth as out of a shrine, as one initiated in the sacred mysteries and filled with the spirit of God. He had himself completely under control, a man guided by reason and stable in his character."[16] After two decades in solitude, not only his body but his soul had become stronger than ever, and he was ready to begin the last great stage of his life, which would reveal him to be truly "Anthony the Great" and "The Father of Monks."

---

[16]   Ibid., 14.

CHAPTER FIVE

Father of Monks

Having emerged from his solitude, Anthony was ready to share with others the wisdom he had accumulated by long experience and strenuous effort. Athanasius says, "Anthony exhorted and advised" the crowd that had gathered to break down the door "to remember the good things to come, and the loving kindness of God towards us. . . . He persuaded many to embrace the solitary life. The desert was colonized," Athanasius continues, "by monks who came forth from their own people, and enrolled themselves for the citizenship in the heavens."[1] At the Outer Mountain, those who remained with Anthony constructed a *laura* of several cells at a short distance from each other. They were close enough to be able to see Anthony and learn from him on a regular basis, but far enough away from each other to give each monk solitude and silence for prayer.

Anthony only left the Outer Mountain to return to the city once, when a persecution broke out under Emperor

---

[1]   St. Athanasius, *The Life of St. Antony*, 14.

Maximinus Daia. Pope Peter of Alexandria, the patriarch of this city, was killed during the persecution, along with many other martyrs. Anthony, now sixty years old, and several of his monks went to Alexandria, about 150 miles away, to give support to those who had been arrested. Anthony yearned for martyrdom, but he did not provoke it. When the martyrs were taken to court, Anthony and the monks accompanied them to give them moral support. The judge, infuriated by the packed courtroom, ordered all the monks out, accusing them of making a public nuisance and criticizing their poor clothing and hygiene. The next morning, Anthony, having washed his clothes so that the judge could not criticize him for smelling like the desert, came and sat in the front row, directly in front of the judge. His presence was a direct challenge to the judge and a support to those who were on trial. Anthony prayed for them throughout the proceedings and accompanied them to the place of execution.

Athanasius comments that, "The Lord was guarding him from being martyred for our own good, and for the good of others." After the trial and execution of the martyrs, Anthony returned to the Outer Mountain, but he had seen during his time in Alexandria that people had started to hold him in high regard. Some of the comments that the monks had made along their journey left him afraid that he would become conceited, so he decided to find another monastery where he was unknown. Perhaps he could travel up the Nile, he thought, to Upper Egypt, to live there in a monastery in obscurity for the rest of his days.

Around the year 313, then, Anthony stood along the banks of the Nile, looking for a boat to take him to Upper Egypt. He heard a voice telling him to turn around, and he saw a caravan of merchants passing by. The voice instructed him to go with that caravan wherever it would take him, and after a three-day journey of seventy miles into the desert, he arrived at what is known as his Inner Mountain. Anthony fell in love with the place at once and determined to spend the rest of his life there. At first, of course, it gave him plenty of time for solitude and prayer. But soon people found him out: first monks from the Outer Mountain came looking for him, followed by crowds of people from all over who sought his intercession and miraculous gifts of healing.

Athanasius tells us that at the Inner Mountain, Anthony worked miracles almost without number. He saw the souls of the dead ascending into heaven, was able to heal people at a distance by his fervent prayers, and exorcized unclean spirits. He answered questions for people not from his own knowledge but with words that he heard in mystical conversations with Christ, the angels, and the saints. During all this, Anthony was able to maintain his humility because of his life of deep prayer, and he encouraged the people who came to him to take the same attitude. As Athanasius says, "Those who are cured learned to thank not Anthony, but God alone."[2] Moreover, Athanasius remarked, "We must not show ourselves skeptical when it is through a man that all these great wonders came to pass. Anthony healed not by giving out commands, but by

---

2   Ibid., 58.

praying, and by calling upon Christ's name, so that it was clear to all that it was not Anthony who did this, but the Lord, showing his loving kindness to men and curing the sufferers through Anthony."[3]

At the Inner Mountain, Anthony was once again tempted fiercely by the demons. One day he was at prayer around three o'clock, and he had a mystical experience in which he was guided aloft by angels. He encountered demons there, in the air, that flew towards him and, one by one, accused him of all the sins that he committed since his birth. In response, Anthony's guardian angel and the angels around him refuted the devils, telling them that they were not allowed to confront him with the sins that he committed before he became a monk, since the asceticism that he had carried out in his time in the desert had already paid the price for those sins. The angels then challenged the demons to try to accuse Anthony of sins that he had committed in the desert, but the demons found themselves unable to do so.

Having returned to his cell, Anthony spent the remainder of that day fasting and meditating on what he had seen in the air. Even after so many decades in the desert, "he was astonished," St. Athanasius says, "to see against how many we battle, and what labors a person has to pass through"[4] in order to live a holy life.

From time to time, Anthony came to the Outer Mountain to visit the monks who still lived there, who had been his disciples in earlier days. But more often he stayed in

---

3   Ibid., 83–84.
4   Ibid., 65.

solitude at the Inner Mountain, leaving it only twice more for the rest of his life. The first occasion happened in 338, when Anthony was eighty-seven years old. He went to Alexandria to assist Bishop Athanasius to refute the Arian heresy, which denied that Jesus was true God as well as true Man. This doctrine, proclaimed by the Council of Nicaea a dozen years previously, was still being contested.

Anthony, who by this time had become very famous not only in the desert but in the major cities as well, came to defend Athanasius publicly and, by his preaching and example, to lend his moral support and credibility to what Athanasius was trying to accomplish. People marveled at his words because they knew that Anthony did not have formal schooling. His wisdom instead came from long hours of meditation. Athanasius relates several other occasions when people passing through the desert, including both Christian and pagan philosophers, put difficult questions to Anthony and marveled at the depth of his answers, gained through deep meditation and long experience.

Anthony's final journey away from the Inner Mountain was around the year 341, when he was about ninety years old. St. Jerome relates an occasion when Anthony started to think that maybe what people were saying was correct: that he really was the greatest monk in the desert, and God answered his thoughts with a revelation about someone even more experienced in the eremitical life than Anthony. Following this inspiration, Anthony went in search of Paul of Thebes, whom we encountered in chapter 1, whom Jerome and generations since have called "St. Paul, the First Hermit."

Recall that Paul had fled to the desert to escape persecution, when his brother-in-law, envious that Paul had inherited all of his parents' property, was preparing to denounce him to the civil authorities. Having run away from home, Paul found a cave with a narrow, hidden entrance. The cave led to a kind of natural atrium, surrounded by cliffs on every side. Inside this enclosure was a spring that came up, providing a pool of clear, cold water, then went back underground again. By the spring grew a palm tree, which had dates on it that he could use for food and palm fronds from which he could weave clothing for himself. Paul made his home here and lived in solitude for the next ninety-seven years.

When Anthony knew that there was someone like that in the desert, he decided to go and meet him. He set out with only a rough idea of the direction he was supposed to take, not knowing when he set out that it would be a three days' journey through the desert. He got lost, and through a few miraculous interventions, the Lord showed him the way. When he arrived at a cliff face and could not find a way to proceed, he noticed a wolf winding its way through the rocks and followed the wolf to the secret entrance that Paul had found so many years before. He was almost to the entrance that led to that atrium when Paul heard him coming and quickly closed up the entrance in front of him. Anthony pleaded for some time to be let in, and at last Paul unsealed the entrance. The two oldest hermits in the desert finally stood face to face. Anthony was 90 years old, and Paul was 113.

The two talked for a while, prayed together, and sat

under the palm tree. At a certain point, a raven landed on the tree with a loaf of bread in its mouth. Anthony was surprised at this, as was Paul: for many decades, a raven had come each day with half a loaf of bread, but today divine providence had sent the bird with bread enough for two. The pair argued for three hours over which one of them should have the honor of breaking the bread; Paul insisted that Anthony was senior to him because of his reputation, but Anthony insisted the honor was due to Paul because of his advanced years. Finally, they decided to each take one end in their hands and pull together. They shared their simple meal and conversed for a while, until Paul asked Anthony to return to his monastery and bring back a cloak that Bishop Athanasius had given to him some years before. Without stopping to ask himself how Paul knew anything about the cloak, Anthony got up right away to do as the holy man asked him.

He made the three-day journey back to the Inner Mountain as quickly as he could, and without stopping to explain things to the other monks, he set out immediately on the return journey. Along the way, he had a vision of Paul's soul ascending into heaven and pushed himself to hasten. Entering the cave, he saw Paul, as he thought, kneeling in prayer; but drawing closer, he saw that Paul was dead.

Anthony was not sure of his next step but was reluctant to leave Paul's body alone. He dragged it out of the cave and set out for the Inner Mountain, but his strength quickly waned and he resigned himself to dying there in the desert alongside Paul. Suddenly he saw two lions running toward him across the desert and thought for sure that his end had come. But when the animals approached, they sniffed at Paul's body, raised their faces to the heavens, and let out a loud roar, and then began to dig a grave in the sand with their paws. Anthony placed Paul's body in the grave, and the lions stood silently at his side as he recited prayers for Paul's blessed repose. The lions filled in the grave, then came to Anthony with heads bowed and waited for him to give a blessing. Anthony had wrapped Paul's body in Athanasius's cloak, and took for himself the tunic and cap that Paul had woven from the leaves of his date palm tree. Jerome relates that Anthony would always wear the tunic and cap on feast days and concludes the story by remarking that he himself, "should the Lord grant him his wish, would far rather choose Paul's tunic, together with his rewards, than the purple robes of kings, together with their punishment."[5]

Anthony died in 356, and Athanasius published his *Life of Saint Anthony* the following year. It spread like wildfire in the ancient world and, for more than a millennium, was the model of that type of literature called hagiography, the biographies of saints. The *Life* includes much more than the basic historical details of Anthony's life, however, and is perhaps most important as a record of Anthony's spiritual teaching. More than a quarter of the ninety chapters of the *Life*, in fact, relate a long discourse on the spiritual life that Anthony gave to the monks at the Outer Mountain. The *Life* is supplemented by seven surviving letters to his fellow monks, dealing with community life and the necessity of fraternal charity. Given Anthony's lack

---

5   Jerome, *Life of St. Paul the First Hermit*, 18.

of schooling, these may have been dictated to a secretary and were later copied many times and shared with monks throughout the region. In addition, thirty-five "sayings" of Anthony are recorded in the *Alphabetikon*, the collection of spiritual stories and advice attributed to various desert *abbas* and *ammas* and commonly known today as the *Apophthegmata Patrum*, or *The Sayings of the Desert Fathers*. Together, these several sources formed the beginning of the corpus of monastic wisdom that has been handed on and meditated over for more than sixteen centuries. Our next chapter will take a closer look at Anthony's spiritual guidance, which remains as relevant for our own time and place as it was in his.

Chapter Six

The Wisdom of Anthony

S t. Anthony's plan for the monastic life, recorded in chapters 16 to 43 of the *Life*, begins with a simple mission statement: "Beginning over each day," Anthony says, "let us increase our zeal."[1] The monk (and hence the saint) is to be formed through daily effort and by persevering. Day by day, choice by choice, he is called to be attentive to God's will and zealous in his pursuit of holiness, without losing heart amid the struggle. Life on earth is short in comparison to heaven, after all, and so the sacrifices that one has to endure, whatever pain and suffering might come, are small compared to the glory awaiting one who can persevere to the end. By holiness in this life, Anthony insists, we are preparing ourselves for eternal life.

Anthony says that one must not grow weary doing what is right, nor become conceited thinking that he is doing something great by his own strength. He urged his monks not to grow careless though they had been pursuing this life for a long time, since he knew from experience that

---

[1]   Jerome, *Life of St. Paul the First Hermit*, 14.

the devil never relaxes his efforts to draw the monk away from his commitments. He exhorts them to be vigilant and never to turn back to what they had left behind. Here he echoes the warning of Christ himself: "No one who puts his hand to the plow and looks back is fit for the kingdom of God" (Lk 9:62). The monastic life requires a complete break from the world, a total commitment to detachment and mortification.

Above all, Anthony is certain, and urges his monks to be certain, that "the accomplishment is within us if we have the will."[2] Anthony knows that if they are in the desert because God wants it, then God himself will give them the grace and strength necessary to do his will. This is characteristic of an Alexandrian way of thinking, as we have seen in Origen's remarks about asceticism and holiness. The spiritual life, from an Alexandrian perspective, is primarily a matter of renewal, of restoring the image and likeness of God in which each human being is created, but that is marred and disfigured by sin. Anthony describes the spiritual life as a process of purification, of getting back to what was there all along, that sin has obscured but could never wipe out.

"So," Anthony says to his monks, "the task is not difficult. If we remain as we were made, we are in the state of virtue, but if we give our minds to base things, we are accounted evil. If the task had to be accomplished from without, it would indeed be difficult, but since this is within us, let us guard ourselves from foul thoughts."[3]

---

2   Ibid.
3   Ibid., 20.

Anthony is not denying the reality of the original sin and its effects, nor the reality of our personal sins. Rather, he is focusing on the power of divine grace to purify the soul from evil and sustain it in doing good.

Anthony notes that this purification happens in stages. "First," he says, "the body must be purified." And this happens through the process of ascesis, training the body with mortification and penance. "First, the body is purified by much fasting, by many vigils and prayers, and by the service which makes a man to be straitened in body, cutting off from himself all the lusts of the flesh."[4] Once the desires of the body are checked, the relationship between the physical and spiritual parts of the person can be restored. "And, taught by the Spirit, the mind becomes our guide to the labors of body and soul, showing us how to purify them. . . . [It] brings back each of the members of the body to its original condition, having nothing in it from the spirit of Satan. And the body is brought under the authority of the mind, being taught by the Spirit."[5]

Next, the soul can regain control over the senses. "For the eyes it sets a rule," Anthony explains, that they may see rightly and purely, and that in them there may be no guile. After that it sets a rule also for the ears, how they may hear in peace, and no more thirst or desire to hear ill speaking, nor about the falls and humiliations of men." This process of purification, reclamation and renewal extends to the powers of the body: "The Spirit teaches the

---

4   St. Anthony, *Letters*, Letter I, in *The Letters of Saint Antony the Great*, trans. Derwas Chitty (Oxford: SLG Press, 1975).

5   Ibid.

tongue its own purity" and roots out the divisive and cruel language that was at once the cause of the soul's sickness and the sign of it. "After this again the Spirit heals the motions of the hands, which once were moved in a disorderly way," providing temptations for the body, and uses them instead "in almsgiving and prayer," rather than greed and selfishness. Then "the Spirit purifies the belly in eating and drinking, for so long as the desires of the soul were active within it, it was never satisfied in its greedy longing for food and drink, and in this way demons made their onslaught on the soul." The Spirit goes on to purify the sexual parts of the body; it "makes peace to the whole body and cuts off from it all passions." Finally, "after all this, it gives to the feet also their purification. At one time they were not making their steps aright according to God, but now the mind, being unified under the authority of the Spirit, effects their purification, that they should walk according to its will."[6]

Certainly such purification and renewal takes time, dedication, and serious effort, including many bodily and spiritual sacrifices. But this ascetical process will be worth it, Anthony says, because of the rewarding outcome which must surely follow. "When the whole body is purified," he explains, "and has received the fullness of the Spirit, it has received some portion of the spiritual body which it is to assume in the resurrection of the just."[7] Here is the goal of every monk, and the purpose of every ascetical practice:

---

[6]   Ibid.
[7]   Ibid.

to share, even a little bit, here on earth, in the life of glory that is promised to us in the resurrection.

As long as we are living in this world, however, Anthony would have us remember that "we still have enemies, powerful and crafty: the wicked demons."[8] Anthony dedicates about one-third of his address to the monks to explaining the nature and strategies of these spiritual enemies, drawing on his own experience dealing with them face-to-face. This part of the address is not meant to frighten the monks but, in fact, to console and encourage them to perseverance in their own battles.

First, he says, they have to know that the demons who tempt us are great in number and of diverse kinds. Each of them has its own goal and comes at us from its own angle. It is likewise important to remember that they were created good, that they were angels first, who rejected God's call to serve him and to serve us. The reason that they are so hostile to human beings, Anthony explains, is that they do not want us to take the place from which they fell. They are jealous of us; as the book of Wisdom says, "Through the envy of the devil, sin entered the world" (Ws 2:24). So, as they see us growing closer in friendship with God, we can expect that their attacks on us will grow stronger.

Anthony points out that the demons have a general plan of attack. They place stumbling blocks in front of us with evil thoughts. Then they try to intimidate us by exaggerating their size and their strength. Recall the story of Anthony's encounter with the demons in the cave, when they came at him in the form of wild beasts and monsters. He

8   *Life of St. Antony*, 21.

fought them off simply by mocking them. "If you had any power, you wouldn't have to make such noise. If you had any power, there wouldn't have to be so many of you." But those who aren't prepared for them will be intimidated when they take on fearful appearances or make a great noise. Anthony is convinced, as the Church has always taught, that the devil has no real power except what God gives him. And most of a demon's power, Anthony suggests, is in his voice: in its ability to make noise, in its ability to deceive.

Anthony also mentions that a demon can sometimes appear as "an angel of light." This is an expression first used by St. Paul (2 Cor 11:14), and in this context it refers to the ways that the demons sometimes tempt a person with seemingly good things: to take on too many devotions at once, for example, or to leave a monastic vocation to take care of a sick relative. However the demons try to delude us, whether by fear or by charm, Anthony urges the monks not to be deceived. "Indeed, note that he who proclaimed he would dry up the sea and seize the whole world cannot hinder our ascetic practices, nor even stop me speaking against him. Wherefore, let us not pay attention to what he may say—he is a plain liar—nor fear his apparitions, for they are lies too."[9]

The demons "simply are cowards," Anthony says, "and deathly afraid of the sign of the Lord's Cross, since it was on the Cross that the Savior stripped them and made an example of them. . . . Let us ever bear in mind that as long as the Lord is with us, our enemies will do us no

---

9   Ibid., 24.

harm."[10] Prudence is still necessary, to be sure, as well as vigilance and perseverance. But the most important part is to remember not to rely on our own strength, but to trust completely in God's protection. Anthony once related a vision he had of the manifold ways in which the devil attacks believers. "I saw the snares that the devil spreads out over the world, and I said, groaning, 'What can get through from such snares?' Then I heard a voice say to me, 'humility.'"[11] On another occasion, he reminded his monks, "Do not think that your progress has been your own work, but understand that you are always helped by some divine power."[12]

Anthony practiced humility in many ways. One story told about him says that "the brothers praised a monk in front of Abba Anthony. When the monk came to see him, Anthony wanted to know how he would bear insults."[13] So Anthony teased him—gently and lovingly, but definitely teased him—and the man immediately broke down and got angry. Seeing that he couldn't bear insults at all, Anthony said to him, "You are like a village, magnificently decorated on the outside, but destroyed from within by robbers."[14] He insisted to his disciples that they grow in this virtue: "My beloved in the Lord, know yourselves," he wrote to his fellow monks. "For they who know themselves know their time; and they who know their time are

---

[10]   Ibid., 35, 42.

[11]   *Alphabetikon,* Anthony 7.

[12]   *Letters*, Letter VI.

[13]   Ibid., Anthony 15.

[14]   Ibid.

able to stand firm and not be moved about. He who knows himself knows God, and he who knows God is worthy to worship him as is right."[15]

We find in Anthony's teaching a deep love for God, along with a sincere love of neighbor. He said on one occasion, "Our life and our death is with our neighbor. If we gain our brother, we have gained God. But if we scandalize our brother, we have sinned against Christ."[16] Because Anthony knew that he was loved by God, he was able to show to those around him the same mercy, patience, and forgiveness that he had received from the Lord. And he insisted that the monks who were with him do the same, echoing the words of St. John the Evangelist: "If anyone says, 'I love God,' but hates his brother, he is a liar; for whoever does not love a brother whom he has seen cannot love God whom he has not seen" (1 Jn 4:20).

Writing to one of the monasteries near the Outer Mountain, Anthony says that the devil has many ways to tempt us by ourselves, but even more effective are the temptations that he uses on a community. "All the anger, and mutual slander . . . the self-justifications in what we do . . . the contempt . . . when we are bitter against each other with our hard words, grieving at every hour, accusing each other and not ourselves . . . sitting in judgment . . . make us slaves of the demons."[17] When the devil is able to get into a community and disrupt it from within, once the

---

15   St. Anthony, *Letters*, 4.
16   *Alphabetikon*, Anthony 9.
17   St. Anthony, *Letters*, 6.

house is divided, he can conquer each member of it more effectively.

For all of Anthony's personal asceticism, he was prudent in how he imposed it upon himself and others, and could be very gentle when necessary. A story is told in the *Alphabetikon* that one day a hunter came riding by to see him, and found Anthony in a position he did not expect: he and some of the monks from the monastery were sitting and enjoying themselves, sharing a small meal together, and laughing. The hunter was scandalized. He said to himself, "Is this the great Anthony that I've heard so much about? Is this the great Anthony who does so much penance?" He rode up to Anthony and asked him, "How can this be? Why are you out here carrying on instead of doing works of penance?"

Anthony responded by asking the hunter, "Put an arrow in your bow and shoot it." The hunter quickly complied. Anthony then told him to shoot another one, which he did. He asked him to do it again, which he did. "Then the old man said, 'Shoot yet again,' and the hunter replied, 'If I bend my bow so much I will break it.' Then the old man said to him, 'It is the same with the work of God. If we stretch the brethren beyond measure they will soon break. Sometimes it is necessary to come down to meet their needs."[18]

Even the times of rest which are necessary require prudence and discernment, lest too much distraction take one away from his vocation. "Just as fish die if they stay too long out of water," Anthony insists, "so the monks who

---

[18]   *Alphabetikon*, Anthony 13.

loiter outside their cells or pass their time with men of the world lose the intensity of inner peace."[19] Such discernment comes from intentionality: a deliberate pursuit of virtue in a particular way. "Whoever hammers a lump of iron, first decides what he is going to make of it: a scythe, a sword, or an axe. Even so, we ought to make up our minds what kind of virtue we want to forger, or we labor in vain."[20] Clarity about our purpose, and intentionality about the way to accomplish it, enables us to pursue the Lord and his will for us wholeheartedly. "Remember him who gives death and life," Anthony urges us. "Hate the world and all that is in it. Hate all peace that comes from the flesh. Renounce this life, so that you may be alive to God. Remember what you have promised God, for it will be required of you on the day of judgment. . . . Test yourselves to see if you are worthy of God. Despise the flesh, so that you may preserve your souls."[21]

As the Father of Monks, Anthony's words and example had a huge impact on the generation that accompanied him into the desert, as well as on the generations that would follow his plan, down to our own day. In the next few chapters, we will learn from more of the Desert Fathers of that first generation.

---

[19]   Ibid., Anthony 10.

[20]   Ibid., Anthony 35.

[21]   Ibid., Anthony 33.

PART THREE

A Garden in the Wilderness

CHAPTER SEVEN

The Words of the Fathers

O ur knowledge of the desert fathers in the West has a great deal to do with St. Benedict, who is credited with being the father of European monastic life. The *Rule of Saint Benedict* is a work of literary and spiritual greatness in its own right, but Benedict did not want his monks to rely only on his own insights. At the end of his *Rule*, he advised them to draw from several important sources for their spiritual enrichment.

"For those who would hasten to the perfection of that life," he says, "there are the teaching of the holy Fathers, the observance of which leads to the height of perfection." By "holy Fathers," he means not only the Desert Fathers but also the apostles and evangelists, the bishops of the early church, and other theologians. "For what page or what utterance of the divinely inspired books of the Old and New Testaments is not a most unerring rule for human life," he asks, "or what book of the holy Catholic Fathers"—here he means the bishops of the early Church who wrote in response to heresies—"does not loudly proclaim how we may come by a straight course to our Creator? . . . Then the *Conferences* and the *Institutes* [referring to the works of John Cassian] and the *Lives of the Fathers*, as also the rule of our holy father Basil— what else are they but tools of virtue for right-living and obedient monks? But for us who are lazy and ill living and negligent, they are a source of shame and confusion."[1]

Ascetical literature has been handed down in various configurations. One of them we've talked about already, the *vitae* or "Lives" of the Fathers. These are not always strict biographical accounts in the sense of just providing historical details but also provide us spiritual context showing how a vocation was present in a person's life, usually from a very early age. They also often contain discourses or homilies or other records of the teachings of these famous men and women.

A second type of desert literature we might call travel journals, often known as the "Histories." In the second and third generations of desert monasticism, roughly between 360 and 430, there were various people like Rufinus and John Cassian who traveled around the Egyptian desert and recorded their observations of what they found there. Again, the geographical details are not as important as their recollections of the conversations that they had with the monks that they encountered. These journals and histories sometimes contain biographical anecdotes, but mostly they comprise recollections of conversations between the author and the monks.

When John Cassian compiled the *Conferences*, for

---

[1]   *Rule of Saint Benedict*, no. 73.

example, the conversations were recorded forty years after his original visit. So we are dealing not with a direct "stenographic" record as much as Cassian's recollection after a period of much reflection and, as he says explicitly, adaptation to his own local circumstances. So, these second and third generation histories and travel journals go through a period of adaptation and modification from the original source, but they can still be a valuable source of insight for us into what was current in the desert in the time of Cassian's travels.

A third type of ascetical literature are the monastic rules. I've already quoted from the *Rule of Saint Pachomius*, who was the first to put together a monastery in the sense that we think of one today: many buildings together housing many hundreds of monks with a wall around it and a daily schedule of life. He was the first (but certainly not the last) to compose a rule with a schedule of life and basic plans for jobs and organization within the monastery. In addition to these basic plans for living, a monastic rule also contained quotations and reflections on the Scriptures, because the goal of a monastic rule was not just to organize day-to-day activities but to give the monks a reason and an example of how to live like Christ.

Another category of ascetical literature is what we might call works of ascetical theology, books like the *Institutes of the Coenobia,* written by St. John Cassian, or *The Ladder of Divine Ascent,* by St. John Climacus. These are systemized reflections on the lessons that were learned by the desert monks. These are in sharp contrast to the fifth category of literature, the "Sayings of the Fathers," known in Greek as *apophthegmata.* This unusual word is derived from the Greek word *phthegma,* which means "a voice." From there we get *phthengomai,* which means "to utter a sound," and *apophthengomai,* which means "to express an opinion." Finally we arrive at *apophthegmata,* which means "short sayings."

Why all this Greek? Well, because the word *phthegma* is a peculiar word to use for a human voice. It is common in another context, however: that of the barnyard. A *phthegma* often refers to a sound uttered by an animal: an oink, a moo, or a bark is also a *phthegma.* Using a term like *apophthegmata* to refer to the Sayings of the Fathers was a deliberate choice to indicate that these words were short and direct, applied to a particular situation, rather than systemized and formal. They are brief sayings specific to an occasion or a particular need, and often directed at a particular person. They were usually asked for in a specific context, in a very particular way. For example, *The Sayings of the Fathers* gives us this story:

"A monk once came to Basil of Caesarea and said, 'Speak a word, Father.' Basil replied, 'You shall love the Lord your God with all your heart,' and the monk went away at once."[2] We recognize this "word" as a line from the Gospel, but it's not even the whole line. As St. Matthew records, "A scholar of the law tested him by asking, 'Teacher, which commandment in the law is the greatest?' He said to him, 'You shall love the Lord, your God, with all your heart, with all your soul, and with all your mind. This is the greatest and the first commandment. The

---

2   *Sayings of the Fathers,* Basil.

second is like it: You shall love your neighbor as your-self. The whole law and the prophets depend on these two commandments" (Mt 22:45–40). However, the monk left right away, after hearing just the first phrase of this quotation from the Gospel.

The purpose of his going away was to meditate on this "word," this short phrase from the Gospel. The monks in the desert used the expression of *ruminating* on the word, "chewing it over," and continually bringing it back to mind, like a cow chewing the cud. So, when Basil saw the man depart, he didn't stop him. The monk had received his word, and he took it home to reflect on it, to ruminate on it. The idea was that he would come back when he thought that he understood it and was able to put it into practice.

The story goes on: "Twenty years later, he came back and said, 'Father, I have struggled to keep your word. Now, speak another word to me.' And [Basil] said, 'You shall love your neighbor as yourself,' and the monk returned in obedience to keep that word also."[3] The story ends there, leaving us to understand that the monk never came back. The second part of the Great Commandment was enough for him to meditate on for the rest of his life.

As we consider the Sayings of the Desert Fathers, we would do well to take the same approach. Rather than read through many of them quickly, we ought to take a word or story and consider it slowly, meditating on it until we have really understood it and are able to put it into practice, even if it takes a very long time. As we consider each

---

3   Ibid.

saying, moreover, we need to understand that some advice was specific to a particular monk and would not apply to others. An important story from the desert will illustrate the necessity of this approach:

On one occasion, we read in the *Alphabetikon*, "Abba Poemen asked Abba Joseph, 'What should I do when the passions attack me? Should I resist them, or let them enter?' The old man said to him, 'Let them enter and fight against them.'"[4] Abba Poemen returned to his monastery, and another brother came to visit from the monastery where Abba Joseph was living. Abba Poemen was sitting within earshot of the visitor, and heard him say to someone, "Abba Joseph said I ought not to allow the passions the smallest entry into me, but cut them off completely." Now, Abba Poemen started to think about how Abba Joseph told him to let the passions in, and how this caused him a lot of trouble. He was constantly fighting these temptations, having to make sacrifices and do battle with them. And yet this other monk had been told by Abba Joseph to shut them out, and he seemed to have it easier as a result.

So Abba Poemen, very upset, went back to see Abba Joseph. He said, "Abba Joseph, I consulted you about my thoughts and you said one thing to me, and then this other monk came to you and you said a different thing to him." Abba Joseph looked at him and said, "Do you not know that I love you? . . . And did you not say to me, 'Speak to me as you speak to yourself?' . . . Truly, if the passions enter you and you fight them, then you become stronger. I

---

4   Ibid., Joseph of Panephysis, 3.

spoke to you as to myself. But there are others who cannot profit in this way."[5] In other words, Abba Joseph was asking Abba Poemen to trust both his good judgment and his knowledge of Abba Poemen's strengths and needs, and to understand that he tailored his advice to meet the situation of each person who consulted him.

The sayings of the fathers, the *apophthegmata*, come to us in various sources, but the majority are contained in two Greek manuscript collections. One, the *Alphabetikon* from which we have quoted several times already, collects anecdotes and sayings attributed to 128 men and 3 women, presenting them under the names of each in alphabetical order. The other, the *Systematikon*, collects sayings from various abbas and ammas, many of them anonymous, and arranges them by topic, on various themes of the spiritual and ascetical life. Both collections originated in oral traditions, in the ways that the sayings were related from the original *abba* to his disciple(s), who then passed them on to the next generation. They were first committed to writing in the sixth century, and have been copied, rearranged, and recompiled many times since.

The way that the *apophthegmata* became known to the western part of the Church during the Middle Ages was mostly through Latin translations. Pelagius the Deacon compiled a translation known as the *Verba seniorum* (the "Words of the Elders") in Rome around the year 550. This is the translation used by Benedict and other Catholic writers in Europe down through the Middle Ages and the Renaissance. John Moschus, writing in Jerusalem around

---

5   Ibid.

the year 600, put together his own collection called the *Pratum Spirituale* ("The Spiritual Meadow") which has some sources in common with Pelagius and also includes stories from the monks in Palestine and Syria. Paul Evergetinos, the founder of a monastery in Constantinople called the *Theotokos Evergetis*, Our Lady the Benefactress, compiled another important collection that includes the sayings of the Fathers as well as some more systemic teachings and is known as the *Evergetinos* after its compiler. This was put together in Greek around the year 1050 and first published in book form in 1783. Around the same time, Nicodemus of the "Holy Mountain," Mount Athos in Greece, put together a Greek text called the *Philokalia* which includes many writings of the Desert Fathers as well as writings on ascetical spirituality by some later Greek writers.

Nearly a thousand sayings appear in the *Alphabetikon*, attributed to 131 *abbas* and *ammas*. The majority of these individuals are only remembered by a few sayings and are not mentioned in the histories or other documents. On the other hand, more than half of the sayings in the manuscript are attributed to a group of ten monks, each with more than thirty sayings to their name. The *apophthegmata* of Abba Poemen the Great, who appeared in the earlier story of Abba Joseph, comprise about one-fifth of the whole collection.

In the course of the next two chapters, we'll consider four of the Desert Fathers who figure prominently in the *Alphabetikon*: Abba Macarius the Great, Abba Arsenius the Great, Abba Poemen the Great, and Abba John the

Short (who was also pretty great.) These were all spiritual sons, in a manner of speaking, of St. Anthony. Their monasteries were located not far from his, and in the process of learning from him and developing their own experience and spirituality in the desert, they have left us a rich heritage in their sayings and stories in the *Alphabetikon*. They're not the subject of long biographies, but through their sayings, they nevertheless have made a lasting impact on the Church and the world.

CHAPTER 8

St. Arsenius and St. Macarius

St. Arsenius the Great

Arsenius was born in Rome in the year 360. He was well-educated and became a tutor to the children of Emperor Theodosius I. In the fourth century, the empire was divided, and Theodosius spent most of his time in Constantinople, where Arsenius lived in the palace with the emperor and his family. He left the palace, though, and sailed to Alexandria in the year 394. There, he became a disciple of St. John the Short at the monastery in Sketis. He later left Sketis to become a hermit at Petra, not far from there, where he became renowned for his austerity and silence.

We can get a sense of how much silence meant to Abba Arsenius from a story about him in the *Alphabetikon*. One day, Arsenius happened upon some brothers living near a marsh where some reeds were growing. These reeds were blowing in the wind. "The old man said to the brother, 'What is this movement?' They said, 'Some reeds.' Then the old man said to them, 'When one who is living in silent prayer hears the song of a little sparrow, his heart no longer experiences the same peace. How much worse it is when you hear the movement of those reeds.'"[1]

This rather mysterious saying really could only be uttered by St. Arsenius. What difference would it make if brothers were living next to some reeds blowing in the wind? How much noise could they really make? But the fact that Arsenius was so concerned about this little bit of noise has more to do with where he was coming from than where these brothers happened to be living at the time.

Arsenius's early life, we are told, was really anything but silent. When he was living in the palace, he was surrounded by great luxury, many parties, many banquets, so much enjoyment. But he was looking for a way to have a deeper life. In prayer, he told his disciples, he was instructed by God to flee from men. "While still living in the palace, Abba Arsenius prayed to God in these words, 'Lord, lead me in the way of salvation.' And a voice came to him saying, 'Arsenius, flee from men, and you will be saved.'"[2] The *Alphabetikon* continues: "Having withdrawn to the solitary life he made the same prayer again and he heard a voice saying to him: 'Arsenius, flee, be silent, pray always, for these are the source of sinlessness.'"[3]

Through many years of solitude in Sketis, living eventually as an anchorite all by himself, he became renowned for his commitment to a most austere silence, a practice

---

[1]   *Alphabetikon*, Arsenius 25.
[2]   Ibid., Arsenius 1.
[3]   Ibid., Arsenius 2.

that made him seem forbidding to his fellow monks and discouraged some people who came to see him. So sensitive was he to the importance of silence that he had learned how even a small noise, such as reeds blowing, could disturb a person trying to focus entirely on communion with God.

Interestingly, when Arsenius asks about the reeds blowing, he asks about the source not of the noise but of the *movement*. In the writings of the Desert Fathers, this term, *movement*, is used in other contexts to refer to temptations and passions that come from various sources. St. Anthony, for example, says that there are different kinds of movements that affect the soul: they can come from God, from the body, from the emotions or the intellect, or from the devil. The reason that a monk sought solitude in the desert was to provide an atmosphere in which to recognize, root out, and overcome the movements of self-will and the temptations of the demons. To understand the movements that became obstacles between the monk and God, to be committed to this task and to do it well, required a total commitment, such that even the intermittent song of a sparrow would be too great a disruption. For the monks to live in constant proximity to the noise of the reeds, at least in Arsenius's opinion, would make their task of prayer and reflection that much more difficult.

Arsenius's comment on their choice of a home meant that he wanted these monks to be totally committed to perfection and that he thought that they had chosen their place because they weren't paying attention to what the life of a monk really involved. He wanted them to consider again whether they understood what they were doing and whether they could do it in that place or needed to move to somewhere else.

The particular phrasing of this saying from Abba Arsenius, where he refers to "reeds blowing in the wind," brings to our mind also the question that Jesus put to the crowds concerning John the Baptist. Jesus says to them in Luke's Gospel, "What did you go out to the desert to see? A reed swayed by the wind?" (Lk 7:24). When Arsenius questions the monks who placed themselves so close to what he considered an almost constant disturbance, he seems to be asking them the same question, "Why did you come out into the desert? What are you here to do? What are you trying to accomplish?" If they came out to seek solitude and silence, then perhaps they've chosen the wrong place to do it. If it were not for the sake of silence that these brothers came out to the desert, then Abba Arsenius seems to think that they should not have come out to the desert at all.

Following this possible biblical connection to John the Baptist gives us another insight into Abba Arsenius and his situation. In Luke's Gospel, Jesus goes on to talk about John the Baptist in this way: "Then what did you go out to see? Someone dressed in fine garments? Those who dress luxuriously and live sumptuously are found in royal palaces" (Lk 7:25). Those who talk about Abba Arsenius tell us that "it was said of him that, just as none in the palace had worn more splendid garments than he when he lived there, so no one in the Church wore such poor clothing."[4]

---

[4]   Ibid., Arsenius 4.

Arsenius's former life, clothed in soft garments in the court of the emperor, makes a sharp contrast with the asceticism that he had undertaken in the desert. Once he decided to follow the Lord's call, like John the Baptist, he went into the desert and put aside all of his former comforts in order to commune with God in silence. Arsenius is transformed by this experience, and now he also can stand before these monks as a prophet, and more than a prophet. Like St. John the Baptist did so many years before, he calls them to reform their lives.

Arsenius's penance was not always understood or appreciated by those who came to see him in the desert. Like all the monks in the desert, Abba Arsenius would do manual labor. He would gather palm leaves and braid them together in order to make baskets and other crafts that would sometimes be taken into the town and sold so that he and the monks could buy the few supplies that they needed. Water was used to soak the leaves to make them soft enough to plait together, and "it was said of Abba Arsenius that he only changed the water for his palm leaves once a year."[5] Of course, soaking the leaves in the water would create a very bad smell, as the vegetable material in the water would start to decay.

An old man came to see him one day, sat with him for a while to talk and pray with him, and he noticed this bad smell that permeated his small cell. He asked him, "Abba Arsenius, why don't you change the water? You're certainly allowed to change it when it starts to smell bad." Abba Arsenius looked at him and explained that, in the

---

5   Ibid., Arsenius 18.

emperor's palace, he had many beautiful things, including incense and rich fragrances and ointments. "Instead of the perfumes and aromatics that I used in the world," he said, "I must bear this bad smell" as a penance.[6]

Abba Arsenius realized that all the comforts that he had relied on, whether clothing, or perfumes, or rich foods, or other luxuries that he had in the world, had become obstacles to his loving God more deeply and hearing God's word more clearly. In the desert, he overcame these obstacles by deliberately giving them up, voluntarily sacrificing them, and even going to the other extreme to remind himself never to go back and look for them again.

Arsenius did not speak a great deal about his former life, and as a result, sometimes monks who did not know the whole story misunderstood him. The *Alphabetikon* relates that "once, when Abba Arsenius was ill at Sketis, the priest came to take him to church and put him on a bed with a small pillow under his head. An old man who was coming to see him saw him lying on a bed with a little pillow under his head and he was shocked," because he misperceived it as luxury. The priest took the monk aside and asked him about his own former life in the world, where he had been a shepherd. "And how did you live?" the priest asked. "I had a very hard life," the monk responded. "And how do you live in your cell now?" the priest inquired. The monk replied, "I am more comfortable." "While you were in the world as a shepherd," the priest explained to the monk, "you did not enjoy even the comforts you have now, but he no longer enjoys the delicate life he lived in the world.

---

6   Ibid.

So you are comforted while he is afflicted."[7] This insight reminded the monk not to judge by outward appearances but to understand that the important thing before God was one's commitment to continual conversion.

Abba Arsenius was committed to living a life of solitude and withdrawing as much as possible from other people. Even when the archbishop of Alexandria wanted to see him and seek his advice on important matters, he sent word to him as follows: "If you come, I shall receive you; but if I receive you, I receive everyone, and I shall no longer live here."[8] He was very concerned to keep his ascetical life as much as possible separated from anything that could draw him back to the way that he had lived in the world.

So we see that Abba Arsenius's commitment to silence was something that he tried to live out every day, and that when he spoke to those monks, he was inviting them also to make a place in their hearts that belonged only to God. This advice applies to us as well. We need to make a place in our hearts, in our day, in our home, in our schedule, in our priorities, where God can come and dwell, a place that belongs only to God. We need a place where we can silence the movements that distract us from God and listen to his word that leads us to a deeper purity of heart.

St. Macarius the Great

Born about sixty years before Abba Arsenius, Abba Macarius the Great was a camel driver who traded in nitre

---

[7]   Ibid., Arsenius 36.
[8]   Ibid., Arsenius 8.

(potassium nitrate or sodium nitrate), a mineral that was mined and used for cleaning clothes and other household tasks. At one point, he was ordained a priest and lived in solitude on the outskirts of his village. St. John Cassian says that Macarius was the first to find a way to inhabit the desert at Sketis. However, he arrived at Sketis under unusual circumstances, though he was never ashamed to tell his story.

The *Alphabetikon* relates that a young woman in the town where Macarius lived had committed fornication and became pregnant. When her parents found out that she was pregnant, they were furious. She didn't want to get her boyfriend into trouble, and so when they asked her who the father was, she blamed the priest Macarius. The townsfolk came and seized him and led him to the assembled people of the village. And as he tells it, they "hung pots black with soot and various other things around my neck. They led me through the village in all directions beating me . . . and they beat me almost to death. The girl's parents said, 'Do not let him go until he has given a pledge that he will take care of her.'"[9]

Macarius knew he was not responsible, but out of compassion for the girl's predicament, he did not say a word. He went to his house with the whole village thinking that he had committed this terrible deed. A friend of his who used to bring him supplies and food told everyone that he hadn't done it, but the villagers didn't believe him. Macarius took up work making baskets. He gave them to his friend and told him, "Sell them and give my wife

---

[9]   Ibid., Macarius 1.

something to eat." Then Macarius said, "I said to myself, 'You have found yourself a wife, you must work a little more in order to keep her.'"

So he worked day and night making baskets and other crafts, giving them to his friend and having him sell them so that he could send money to this girl to keep her in good health until her baby would come. He didn't expose her lie, and he didn't defend himself. When the time came for her to give birth, God seemed to speak for Macarius's innocence. The girl remained in labor for five days and was unable to give birth until finally she said, "I lied, it was not Macarius," and told everyone who the father of her child was. She then gave birth to a healthy child, and the villagers realized their terrible mistake. Macarius concludes the story: "Then the man who served me came here full of joy, saying, 'The whole village wants to come here solemnly and do penance before you.' But when I heard this, for fear people would disturb me, I got up and fled here to Sketis. That is the original reason why I came here."[10]

After many years, when he had become the spiritual father of the monks at Sketis, and everyone came to him for advice, some friends of his from a different monastery came and said to him, "Father, say a word to the brothers." Although he was renowned for his holiness and everyone looked to him for guidance, he gave them what they all considered a rather unusual response. He said to them, "I have not yet become a monk, but I have seen monks."[11]

---

[10]   Ibid.

[11]   Ibid., Macarius 2.

They thought, "How can he say that he had not yet become a monk? He is the holiest among us."

So he told them the story: One day, when trying to get away from the monastery for a little while, he had gone deeper into the desert where he found two hermits living among the animals and drinking at an oasis. They told him they depended totally on God for safety, shelter, and food, and had lived in complete solitude away from the world for forty years.

"I asked them, 'How can I become a monk?' They said to me, 'If you do not give up all that is in the world, you cannot become a monk.' I said to them, 'But I am weak; I cannot do as you do.' They said to me, 'If you cannot become like us, sit in your cell and weep for your sins.'"[12] Upon his return to the monastery, Macarius renewed his commitment to silence and contemplation, striving to follow the word of the two monks he found in the deep desert. But he knew how much more he had to grow, and for that reason responded that he was "not yet a monk." His humble admission is a reminder and a challenge for anyone trying to live the spiritual life. As much as we are trying to make progress, we still have to rely on God for help and still consider ourselves beginners with many things to learn and much progress still to make.

Abba Macarius was renowned for his detachment from material goods, and several interesting stories from his time at Sketis tell us just how detached he could be. On one occasion, he had gone out from his cell to pray or to work. He came back and found someone robbing him,

---

12   Ibid.

loading all of Macarius's few possessions onto a beast of burden. "So he came up to the thief as if he were a stranger and he helped him to load the animal. He saw him off in great peace of soul, saying, 'We have brought nothing into this world, and we cannot take anything out of the world' (1 Tm 6:7)."[13]

Another time something similar happened. Macarius came back to his cell to find a man loading up his few possessions onto his camel. When the man tried to leave, the camel wouldn't move. Macarius went into his cave and found a small garden implement that he used to plant a few vegetables on which he lived. He came out and said to the robber, "The camel wants you to take this too." He loaded it up, but the camel still wouldn't go. "Then the old man kicked the camel, saying, 'Get up.' At once it got up and went forward a little, because of his command. Then it lay down again and refused to get up until it was completely unloaded, and then it set off."[14]

These stories are interesting for another reason: because of the reputation that Macarius had during his days in the world. We have seen that he sold nitre, but some people said that he had actually stolen it and resold it, and that was how he made his money. Most monks and visitors would have considered it highly disrespectful to mention this to him. But the *Alphabetikon* relates, "If one of the brethren said to him, as though to humiliate him, 'Abba, when you were a camel-driver and stole nitre and sold it again, didn't the keepers beat you?' If someone talked to

---

13   Ibid., Macarius 18.
14   Cf. ibid., Macarius 40.

him like that, then he would talk to them with joy about whatever they asked him."[15] He tried to avoid people that treated him as someone special, instead preferring those who would give him a chance to be humble, those who didn't take him too seriously. He loved to see people who would speak to him as an ordinary man, and he was not embarrassed by them if they gave him a reason to stay humble.

This humility gave him great power over the devil. It's said that one time, when he was coming back to his cave after having gotten a little bit of water from the marsh, he had a vision of the devil who walked up to him and said, "What is your power, Macarius, that makes me powerless against you? All that you do, I do, too. You fast, so do I. You keep vigil, and I do not sleep at all. In one thing only do you beat me. Your humility. Because of that, I can do nothing against you."[16] Because Macarius was humble, he was able not only to conquer the demon himself but also to help others to do the same.

One more story will show us how gentle he was with others who had struggles against temptations. As he was sitting by his cell one day, he saw the devil coming over the hill and going down to the monastery nearby. The devil was wearing a garment full of pockets with little bottles in them. Macarius asked him, "What's all that?"

The devil said, "Well, I'm going down to the monastery where many brothers are dwelling. In these bottles

---

[15]   Ibid.
[16]   Ibid., Macarius 11.

are temptations. I carry many of them because I can tempt them sometimes with one, sometimes with another."

Then, when the evil one returned, Macarius said, "Well, how did it go?" The demon replied, "Everyone down there resists me except for one brother. I never have to try more than two or three of these, and I can always find a friend in him." Macarius asked who it was that the devil was able to get the best of. Then he went down to the monastery and asked to see that man, whose name was Theopemptus.

"When he was alone with him, the old man asked him, 'How are you getting on?' Theopemptus replied, 'Thanks to your prayers, all goes well,' The old man asked: 'Do not your thoughts war against you?' He replied, 'Up to now, it is all right," for he was afraid to admit anything." Macarius had a plan for helping the monk to speak freely, "The old man said to him, 'See how many years I have lived as an ascetic, and am praised by all, and though I am old, the spirit of fornication troubles me.' Theopemptus said, 'Believe me, abba, it is the same with me.' The old man went on admitting that other thoughts still warred against him, until he had brought him to admit them about himself."[17] They went on to discuss Theopemptus's spiritual regimen, and Macarius offered some advice and suggested some adjustments. Then he returned to his cell.

Soon after, Macarius had another vision of the devil coming back from that monastery. He asked him what success he had had, and the demon admitted that it had gone badly. "The worst," he complained, "is the one friend I had who used to obey me. I do not know what has

17   Ibid, Macarius 3.

changed him, . . . but he has become the most stubborn of them all. So I have promised myself not to go down there again for a long time."[18]

---

[18]   Ibid.

CHAPTER NINE

St. John and St. Poemen

St. John the Short

Abba John of Sketis was born about 339, the son of poor parents in the village of Tessa. He went to Sketis at the age of eighteen and was trained by Abba Ammonas for about twelve years. Later, he attracted many disciples to Sketis, including Abba Arsenius. In order to preserve his solitude as more and more people came to Sketis and asked to be his disciples, he dug a cave underground where he could retreat from time to time. He was later ordained a priest, and the *Alphabetikon* records forty-seven sayings from Abba John. Around the year 395, he left Sketis and retreated to the Inner Mountain, where St. Anthony had lived.

The most famous story about Abba John comes from when he first arrived at Sketis and put himself under the direction of Abba Ammonas. "It was said of Abba John that he withdrew and lived in the desert at Sketis with an old man. His abba, taking a piece of dry wood, planted it and said to him, "Water it every day with a bottle of water until it bears fruit." Now the water at Sketis was so far away from where John had made his little dwelling that he had to leave in the evening and sleep there overnight and return with the water in the morning. Nevertheless, John carried out this instruction of his abba every day for three years. At the end of three years, the story goes, the wood sprouted. First leaves started to grow on it, then flowers, and then it bore fruit. Abba Ammonas took the fruit from the tree, carried it to the church where the monks at Sketis gathered each weekend for common prayers, and gave it to the assembled brethren, saying, "Take and eat the fruit of obedience."[1]

John was renowned in his day for this marvelous obedience and humility, but this did not come automatically. When John arrived in Sketis at the age of eighteen, it was not the first time that he had tried to be a monk. On a previous occasion he said to his older brother, "I want to be free of all care. I want to live like the angels, who don't work, but ceaselessly offer their prayers to God." So he took off his cloak and he left for the desert. He lasted for a week and then he came home to his brother's house.

When he knocked on the door, he heard his brother inside, who said, "Who are you?" He said, "I'm John. I'm your brother." But from inside, his brother said, "John? I thought John has become an angel. John doesn't live among men anymore." His brother didn't let him inside, even though John pleaded. His brother left him on the doorstep in distress until the morning and finally opened

---

[1]   *Alphabetikon*, John the Short 1.

the door and said, "Oh, well now you are a man again, aren't you? Well you have to work again in order to eat." So John made a prostration on the doorstep and asked for forgiveness.

John then realized that the desert life had to mean a total commitment. He had to think it through before he did it, and make sure that this was really his vocation. It wasn't something that could be tried for a while every so often. He went to Sketis after he had discerned that it was indeed what God wanted from him, and that he was ready to do it for his entire life, and we find from his own words that he went to Sketis because he realized that he needed to be there. When someone asked him why he had gone to the desert, John replied, "I am like a man sitting under a great tree, who sees wild beasts and snakes coming against him in great number. When he cannot withstand them any longer, he runs to climb the tree and is saved. It is just the same with me. I sit in my cell and I am aware of evil thoughts coming against me, and when I have no more strength against them, I take refuge in God by prayer and I am saved from the enemy."[2]

Of course, when he talked about this great tree, Abba John must have had in mind the tree of the cross. He came to Sketis because he needed to get as close as possible to the Savior, to have constant access to God and to divine grace. So he separated himself as much as he could from the things of the world, from any distractions that could become an obstacle between him and Jesus Christ, and he learned not to trust in himself but always to rely on God in

[2]   Ibid., John the Short 12.

the struggle. Again, this wasn't something that happened automatically in his life but something that he learned from experience.

Abba Poemen, who lived with Abba John, said that on one occasion he found out that Abba John had asked God to take away his temptations so that he might be free from care. He went and told one of the abbas, "I find myself in peace, without an enemy." His abba replied that John had made a serious mistake. "Go, beseech God to stir up warfare in you,"—to give you back your temptations, in other words—"so that you may regain the affliction and humility that you used to have, for it is by warfare that the soul makes progress."[3] Abba John asked God to give him back the temptations that he could handle and that he needed to fight against so that he would remember to be humble. "So he besought God," the story concludes, "and when warfare came, he no longer prayed that it might be taken away, but said, 'Lord, give me strength for the fight.'"[4]

Here we see some parallels, perhaps, to the story in the life of St. Anthony when he was in the tombs outside his village and the devils came to attack him. When the Lord Jesus appeared and Anthony asked where he had been, Jesus told Anthony, "I waited to see how you would fight." He gave Anthony a chance to fight against the demons in order to develop his strength and also to develop his insight into how to fight them and to understand the kinds of tactics that they would use against him. Abba John also had to fight the demons because it was good for him: it

---

3   Ibid., John the Short, 13.

4   Ibid.

taught him where his strength came from and taught him to be humble and to rely on Christ.

We see a similar sentiment in the writings of St. Paul. In his Second Letter to the Corinthians, Paul writes frankly about "a thorn in the flesh" that the Lord permitted him to suffer, "to keep me from being too elated" (2 Cor 12:7). Paul says, "Three times I besought the Lord about this, that it should leave me; but he said to me, 'My grace is sufficient for you, for my power is made perfect in weakness'" (vv. 8–9). Realizing that God had promised to help him bear what he could not bear by his own strength or his own will, Paul was able to "boast of my weaknesses, that the power of Christ may rest upon me. For the sake of Christ, then, I am content with weaknesses, insults, hardships, persecutions, and calamities; for when I am weak, then I am strong" (vv. 9–10).

John the Short came to the same conclusion. By accepting the temptations that the Lord had sent to him, he was able to grow in humility and commitment to the ascetical life. He had also learned not to put himself unnecessarily in the path of distractions and temptations. For example, "It was said of Abba John that when he went to church at Sketis, he heard some of the brethren arguing, so he returned to his cell. He went round it three times, and then went in."[5] Noticing this strange behavior, "some brethren who had seen him wondered . . . and they went to ask him. He said to them, 'My ears were full of that argument, so I circled round in order to purify them, and thus I entered

---

5   Ibid., John the Short 25.

my cell with my mind at rest.'"[6] He knew himself well
enough to know that if he took that distraction with him
into the solitude, that it would bother him, probably all
night long.

This is an important lesson for us as well. If we are
striving to grow in prayer and contemplation, one thing to
keep in mind is how difficult it is to go from the business
of our daily lives to times of prayer. Like Abba John, who
needed to transition from that argument that he heard coming back from the church and get it out of his mind before
he went into the silence, when we come from wherever
we are—from work, from play, from the busyness of our
daily lives—if we are going to pray to God, we need to
prepare our minds and hearts. We need to make a transition from one part of life to another, making sure that we
give ourselves over to the Lord fully and take time to quiet
down and move from one frame of mind to another.

Abba John was very practical in the way that he tried
to prepare himself and others for living a spiritual life.
He said, "A house is not built by beginning at the top and
working down. You must begin with the foundations in
order to reach the top. The foundation is our neighbor,
whom we must win, and that is the place to begin. For all
the commandments of Christ depend on this one."[7] The
love of neighbor was essential for his plan of asceticism.
In fact, it was for him the starting point and it led to what
we might call his spiritual doctrine. Abba John said:

---

[6]   Ibid.

[7]   Ibid., John the Short 39.

I think it best that a person should have a little bit of all the virtues. Therefore, get up early every day and acquire the beginning of every virtue and every commandment of God. Use great patience, with fear and long suffering, in the love of God, with all the fervor of your soul and body. Exercise great humility. Bear with interior distress. Be vigilant and pray often, with reverence, with purity of speech, and control of your eyes. When you are despised, do not get angry. Be at peace and do not render evil for evil. Do not pay attention to the faults of others and do not try to compare yourself with others, knowing that you are less than every created thing. Renounce every material thing and that which is of the flesh. Live by the cross, in warfare, in poverty of spirit, taking hold of that which is good. Do your work in peace. Persevere in keeping vigil, in hunger and thirst, in cold and nakedness, and in sufferings. Shut yourself in a tomb as though you are already dead, so that at all times you will think that death is near.[8]

Such a straightforward approach to the spiritual life is characteristic of John the Short, both in his own actions and in the way he advised others. One more story, though, illustrates just how gentle this plain-spoken man could be, especially with beginners and those who struggled in the spiritual life. An older man in the monastery, who was very penitential with his body but not always very clear in his thoughts, came to see Abba John one day to ask

---

8   Ibid., John the Short 34.

him about forgetfulness. Abba John spoke to him for a while and gave him a word to think about. The old man went back to his cell and promptly forgot what Abba John had said to him. So he came back to ask him, "Remind me, what was that you told me about forgetfulness?" Abba John smiled, and they discussed it again, after which the monk went back to his cell and thought about it and forgot again. He came back to Abba John a second time, then a third and a fourth and a fifth time, and each time Abba John received him again with kindness and reminded him about what he forgot about forgetfulness. Finally, after half a dozen times, the man got embarrassed and decided not to come back.

That weekend when all the monks came for the *synaxis*, the gathering for prayer and for the Eucharist, Abba John saw the forgetful monk and asked why he had not returned for a while. The man admitted that he had gotten embarrassed to ask again. After the prayers were over, they stayed in the sanctuary and Abba John "said to him, 'Go and light a lamp.' He lit it. Then he said to him, 'Bring some more lamps, and light them from the first.' He did so. Then Abba John said, 'Has that lamp suffered any loss from the fact that other lamps have been lit from it?' He said, 'No.' Then the old man continued: 'So it is with John. Even if the whole of Sketis came to see me, they would not separate me from the love of Christ. Consequently, whenever you want to, come to me without hesitation.'"[9]

Because Abba John had become so humble and remembered that everything he had received was from the

---

[9]   Ibid., John the Short 18.

bounteous generosity of Christ, he was able to be generous and patient with others. It may be difficult to imitate
John's radical obedience, watering the dry sticks in our
own lives without question or hesitation. But we may hope
to acquire some of his humility by imitating his generous
availability to those who need our spiritual support and
help, and welcoming them as we would welcome Christ.

St. Poemen the Great

The last of the Desert Fathers that we will consider from
the *Alphabetikon* is the source of 15 percent of the entire
collection. A total of 209 sayings are attributed to him,
leading some scholars to suggest that the original manuscripts of the *Alphabetikon* were compiled by his disciples, and the sayings of the other fathers and mothers were
added to an original collection of Abba Poemen's sayings.

Abba Poemen's name means "the shepherd." He was
one of seven brothers, all of whom went away together
to become monks. They settled near Sketis, which is also
probably where he was born, around the year 370. He
lived until at least the year 450; we know this because he
outlived Abba Arsenius. At Sketis he became acquainted
with St. Anthony, St. Arsenius, St. John the Short, and
many others.

The *Alphabetikon* relates that once, Abba Paesius, the
brother of Abba Poemen, made friends with someone
outside his cell. Abba Poemen was annoyed by this and
didn't want such noise going on. He went to his spiritual
father, Abba Ammonas, to complain about this. His abba's
response was pithy and made an impact: "Poemen, are

you still alive? Go and sit down in your cell. Engrave it on your heart that you have been in the tomb for a year already."[10] This was a challenge to him to realize that it was his responsibility to find his solitude and to act as if nothing could bother him. From that point on, he took his vocation to go into the desert, and to live there as if he were already dead to the world, very seriously.

When his brothers and he were living in Egypt, their mother came to see them. She was not able to do so, because women were not allowed anywhere near the monastery, but she knew where they gathered for prayer. So she ambushed them, waiting for them in the alley near the church. When they saw her, the brothers made a detour down one of the side lanes and got to their cave before she could get there. They closed the door in her face, desiring to make sure that their separation from the world, even from their family, was complete. She cried out through the door, "I want to see you, my children. What's the worst that could happen? What will happen if I do see you? I'm your mother." Abba Poemen said to her, "Would you rather see us here or in the age to come? If you refrain from seeing us now, you will see us there." "So she departed full of joy," the *Alphabetikon* relates, "and said, 'If I shall see you perfectly there, I do not need to see you here.'"[11]

This can seem very harsh to us, that sons should stay so aloof from their family, from their own mother. But then we remember the words of the Scripture, when the Lord Jesus says, "He who loves father or mother more than me

---

[10]   Ibid., Poemen 2.

[11]   Ibid., Poemen 76.

is not worthy of me" (Mt 10:37), and "If any one comes to me and does not hate his own father and mother . . . yes, and even his own life, he cannot be my disciple" (Lk 14:26). All of our relationships must come second to our relationship with God, and the monks of the desert, who needed to be separated completely from all that they had left behind, took this responsibility very seriously.

Abba Poemen insisted that we need fervor in our relationship with God if we will be able to persevere in the ascetical life. "As long as a pot is on the fire," he explained, "neither a fly nor any other animal can get near it. But as soon as it is cold, these creatures get inside. So it is for the monk. As long as he lives in spiritual activities, the enemy cannot find a means of overthrowing him."[12] But when we let our hearts grow cold, then we open ourselves up to temptations. To maintain this fervent devotion, he said, "these things are the most helpful of all: fear of the Lord, prayer, and doing good to one's neighbor. He also said, 'Poverty, hardship, austerity, and fasting, such are the instruments of the solitary life.'"[13] Notice how external penances come second to the internal dispositions of love of God and neighbor. As we have seen, for the desert monks, ascetical practices were never an end in themselves but always a means for supporting and enlivening their commitment to prayer and charity.

Abba Poemen was very realistic about what was possible in the spiritual life, and he encouraged those around him not to take on too much, or try to do too much too

---

[12]   Ibid., Poemen 111.
[13]   Ibid., Poemen 160.

fast. "A brother came to see Abba Poemen and said to him, 'Abba, I have many thoughts and they put me in danger.' The old man led him outside and said to him, 'Expand your chest and do not breathe in.' He said, 'I cannot do that.' Then the old man said to him, 'If you cannot do that, no more can you prevent thoughts from arising, but you can resist them.'"[14] In other words, just as one cannot help breathing in and out, we cannot help but be tempted, because we're in the body and the devil will always find ways to attack us. The important thing is not to resent temptations, or to try to live as if they do not affect us, but to be on our guard, to be prepared and ready to resist them rather than giving in.

Just as patience and realism are required for facing and resisting temptations, Poemen advised patience and moderation regarding penance. "A brother said to Abba Poemen, 'I have committed a great sin and I want to do penance for three years.' The old man said to him, 'That is a lot.' The brother replied, 'For one year?' The old man said again, 'That is a lot.' Those who were present said, "For forty days?' The old man said again, 'That is a lot.' He added, 'I myself say that if a man repents with his whole heart, and does not intend to commit the sin anymore, God will accept him after only three days."[15]

How should one interpret this saying, which seems so lax, especially given the desert monks' reputation for strict asceticism and penance? Surely Abba Poemen had devoted himself to the ascetic life, to repenting of his own

---

[14]   Ibid., Poemen 28.

[15]   Ibid., Poemen 12.

sins and to serving God with an undivided heart, but again we see his concern for prioritizing the internal over the external. Rather than a long period of visible, bodily penance, he was looking for the man to repent "with his whole heart" and to have a firm intention to avoid the sin in the future. If these were in place, Poemen seems to say, then an extended period of bodily fasting and penance would not be necessary. And if the monk had tried to win forgiveness just by this outward penance, without the inward dispositions, even three years of such penance would have been empty and futile.

In these interactions we see how Poemen the solitary lived up to his name, which means "shepherd." His stories and sayings are filled with great compassion for the flock of disciples under his care at Sketis, and he guided them with compassion, gentleness, and patience, even as he called them to repentance and detachment. "A brother asked Abba Poemen, 'How should I behave in the place where I live?' The old man said, 'Have the mentality of an exile in the place where you live, do not desire to be listened to and you will have peace.' He also said, 'This voice cries out to a man to his last breath: *Be converted today.*'"[16] Here is the spiritual task that Poemen sets for all of us: to open our hearts to God's forgiveness, to put away the sins and the temptations and the attachments to the world that may be keeping us from God. Poemen's advice, delivered with such patience and kindness, ought to encourage us to respond to God's call to conversion with sincere hearts.

---

[16]   Ibid., Poemen 191–92.

PART FOUR

St. Syncletica and the Desert Ammas

CHAPTER TEN

The Mothers of the Desert

The *Alphabetikon,* as we have seen, records stories of 128 Desert Fathers, but contains the sayings of only 3 Desert Mothers. This and other records of the Egyptian desert do not exactly give equal time to the contribution that women made to the development of monastic life, and hardly even account for their presence there. An important exception is the *Monastic History* of St. Palladius, often called the *Lausiac History* because it was written for Bishop Lausus. Palladius reports that in Tabennisi, near the monastery of St. Pachomius, there was a monastery of some 400 women, founded by Pachomius's sister. The women who came to live with her, Palladius tells us, "had the same sort of management, and the same way of life" as in Pachomius's own monastery.[1]

Eventually, almost as many women as men lived in the deserts of Egypt and Palestine. Palladius says, "I

---

[1]   Palladius, *The Lausiac History,* trans. Robert T. Meyer, Ancient Christian Writers series, no. 34 (New York: Newman, 1964), 33.1.

must also commemorate the courageous women to whom
God granted struggles equal to those of men, so that no
one could plead as an excuse that women are too weak
to practice virtue successfully. Now I have seen a good
many of them, and I have associated with many refined
women among virgins and widows."[2] Among these he
mentions the Roman matron Paula, "a woman highly distinguished in the spiritual life. . . . She was well able to
surpass everyone else," Palladius notes, "being a genius
of a woman." He also mentions "a woman called Hosia,
a most renowned woman in every way," and "Basianillia
too," who "practiced virtue zealously and carefully, and is
still vigorously fighting the good fight."[3]

Now in many of these cases all we have from Palladius and other sources are names of people—both women
and men—living in the desert. Fortunately, Palladius does
give us some more detail about a few of these extraordinary Desert Mothers. He relates the story of Amma
Alexandra, for example, a housemaid who left a certain
city and walled herself up in a tomb. "She received the
necessities of life through a window," he says, "and for
ten years never looked a man or woman in the face."[4] Why
did she do such a thing? Palladius tells us of a conversation he had with Alexandra, relating her own words: "A
man was distracted in mind because of me. And rather
than scandalize a soul made in the image of God, I betook

---

2   Ibid., 41.1.

3   Ibid., 41.2–4.

4   Ibid., 5.1.

myself alive to a tomb, lest I seem to cause him suffering or reject him."[5]

Here we encounter a somewhat unique reason for fleeing from the world, as Alexandra accepts a life of personal asceticism out of concern for the spiritual good of another. Many monks and nuns went to the desert in order to dedicate their lives to God. Amma Alexandra went and walled herself up in this tomb, not only to give herself to God, but also to save someone else from becoming a sinner. She was willing to accept sacrifices on her own behalf in order to help someone else to be holy.

Palladius also writes about Amma Isadora, under the heading of "The Nun who Feigned Madness." In order to maintain her humility, Isadora pretended to be insane, or to be possessed by a demon. She entered a certain monastery, which took her in, not as a nun, but as a servant. She did the hardest and dirtiest work in the kitchen. She wore a dirty rag around her head, and she never ate with the others, but swept up the crumbs from the table and ate whatever was left. She never grumbled or complained, nor talked to many people, and certainly never treated anyone unkindly. But that attitude was not reciprocated: Isidora was often cursed, insulted, and mistreated by the sisters of the monastery where she lived.

On one occasion, a famous abba named Piteroun was directed by a vision of an angel to visit the monastery where Abba Isadora was living. He had been thinking to himself that he had grown fairly advanced in holiness, and this angelic visitor was sent—like the vision which told

---

[5]   Ibid., 5.2.

St. Anthony about St. Paul of Thebes—to show him that there was someone much holier and much more humble than himself. When he arrived at the monastery, the abbess gathered all the sisters together in the chapel to receive Abba Piteroun. He came in and was greeted very warmly. Looking around, he insisted that the abbess had not called all of the nuns together and that he would not begin until everyone was present. She thought that he could not possibly want to see mad Isidora the kitchen maid, but he insisted. When she came in, Piteroun knelt at her feet and asked for her blessing.

The nuns were shocked, and so Piteroun explained the vision he had received. He related that the angel had told him, "Go to the Tabenna monastery. There you will see a sister wearing a rag on her head. She serves them all with love, and endures their contempt without complaint. Her heart and her thoughts rest always with God. You, on the other hand, sit in solitude, but your thoughts flit about all over the world."[6] At once all of the sisters in the monastery came to ask her forgiveness, and they continued to do so over the next several days. Realizing that she would no longer be able to live there in obscurity and inner peace, one night Isidora left the monastery in secret and disappeared, never to be seen again.

Another of the great women of the desert whom St. Palladius speaks of, who is also one of the three included in the *Alphabetikon*, is Amma Theodora. She was the wife of a tribune, a government official, and therefore a very wealthy woman. But Palladius tells us that she acquired

---

6   Ibid., 34.3–4.

such a depth of poverty once she came to the desert that she actually relied on the alms of others to survive. She eventually died in the monastery of Hesychas near the sea. Among other people, Archbishop Theophilus as well as many monks from nearby monasteries came to ask her advice on the monastic life.

Amma Theodora's approach was quite practical. "Just as trees cannot bear fruit if they have not stood before the winter's storms," she said, "so it is with us. This present age is a storm, and it is only through many trials and temptations that we can obtain an inheritance in the kingdom of heaven."[7] Like Abba John the Short and Abba Poemen, Amma Theodora understood intuitively that temptations can be useful if they teach us to be humble and to rely on God for his strength. They can be a useful training for us and preparation in the spiritual life.

Another amma who appears in the *Alphabetikon*, Amma Sarah, struggled against impure desires, as she admits, for more than thirteen years. She relied on God's strength and not her own; "she never prayed that the warfare should cease, but she said, 'O God, give me strength.'"[8] Finally a demon appeared to her, who identified itself as the demon of lust, and said to her, "You have overcome me." She replied, "It is not I who have overcome you but Christ, my master."[9] She told him that Christ was fighting in her, and fighting for her. It said that she was so careful to keep custody of her eyes, to make sure that she never looked at

---

[7]   *Alphabetikon*, Theodora 2.

[8]   Ibid., Sarah 1.

[9]   Ibid., Sarah 2.

anything that could be a temptation for her, that "for sixty years she lived beside a river and never lifted her eyes to look at it."[10] So intense was her desire for asceticism and detachment that she gave herself over to it completely.

She said about her conduct in the desert, "If I prayed and asked God that all people should approve of my conduct, I would find myself a penitent at the door of each one. I rather pray that my heart will be pure towards all."[11] She knew that it was more important to please God, and to do God's will, than to look for approval from others. She was single-hearted and wanted only to serve God. And she knew that if she did his will, then she would be good towards others. Whether they always understood what she was doing or not, she knew that she couldn't go wrong by following God's commandments.

Amma Matrona was born in Asia Minor in the fifth century. She was married to a very wealthy man and had a daughter with him. The family settled in Constantinople when Matrona was twenty-five. She would spend entire days in church, and began to live a very ascetic life, a life that her husband didn't understand. He was very cruel to her, mocking her asceticism and eventually becoming more violent towards her when she didn't give up on her life of prayer.

In response to a dream, which she took as a sign of God's will, in which she saw herself leaving her house and walking away into the desert, she finally left her husband. She gave her daughter over to the care of the elder women

---

[10]   Ibid., Sarah 3.
[11]   Ibid., Sarah 5.

in church and decided to join a monastery. It was to be a monastery for men, so that her husband would not be able to find her. Of course this would not be allowed, she knew, so she cut her hair, put on men's clothes, and lowered her voice, and entered a men's monastery in secret. She passed her time in silence and in manual labor so as not to give herself away.

On one occasion, one of the monks in the monastery noticed that her ears had holes in them, as she had once had them pierced for earrings. He asked her about this and she simply looked at him and said, "I think it is better in the monastery if everyone attends to his own affairs." He was humbled and left her alone after that. One night the abbot had a dream that revealed that she was in fact a woman, and so she was sent away to a woman's monastery in Amessa, where she became the abbess.

Her husband found out and came after her, which meant that she had to flee from him to Lebanon where she lived in an abandoned temple. Women came to live with her there, and when her husband finally died, all of them moved to Constantinople. She died there at the age of one hundred, after living a life of monasticism for seventy-five years. She said about the monastic life, "We carry ourselves wherever we go, and we cannot escape temptation by mere flight. Many people living secluded lives on the mountain have perished by living like people in the world. It is better to live in a crowd and want to live a solitary life, than to live a solitary life but all the time be longing for company."[12]

---

[12]   Quoted in Laura Swan, *The Forgotten Desert Mothers:*

It is very tempting to believe these monks and nuns who lived all by themselves had it very simple, and how simple our lives could be if we could just get away from everything. Leave the world behind, we think, and automatically we are leaving our troubles behind. Then we wouldn't have anything else to bother us. But wherever we go, Amma Matrona reminds us, we take ourselves with us. We take our memories, our bad habits, our temptations with us, and we still must deal with the part of ourselves that is unconverted. So we need to be able to overcome obstacles, with God's help, and ask for God's grace and forgiveness right where we are.

Amma Syncletica

One of the most famous women of the desert, known as well in the Western part of the Church as in the East, is the woman known as Amma Syncletica. Her name is perhaps not a household name to us, and it is a rather unusual name as well. But it has a deep symbolic significance. In Greek, a *synkletos* is an assembly. Her biographer, known as Pseudo-Athanasius, suggests that even from her birth, God was preparing her to be numbered among the *synkletos*, the assembly, of the saints in heaven. It could have another meaning: in the ancient world, *synkletos* was also the name of the legislative body we would call a senate. It is possible that Syncletica was the daughter of a senator or another important person in her community.

Syncletica was born in Alexandria, Egypt, around

Sayings, Lives and Stories of Early Christian Women (New York: Paulist Press, 2001), 35.

the year 270. Her parents were not Egyptians but rather
from Macedonia. They were fairly well to do, and they
immigrated to Alexandria because of the reputation of the
Christians there. In her very distinguished family, there
were four siblings: she had a sister, who was blind, and
two brothers. One of her brothers died in childhood, and
the other brother lived until the age of about twenty-five.
Her parents had arranged a marriage for him when he
came of age, but he died just before his marriage was
about to take place. Syncletica was, by all accounts, a
very holy child, and also very beautiful. Because of this,
and because her family was very wealthy and influential
in their community, she had many suitors. Her parents
encouraged her to marry, especially because she was their
only hope of grandchildren: her blind sister had little hope
of being married, and by this time, both her brothers had
passed away.

Syncletica ignored those who came to seek her hand
in marriage and, in fact, neglected her appearance so as
to discourage them. She desired a divine marriage, a total
commitment to Christ. Among those who knew her, and
by her biographer as well, this was considered a new kind
of martyrdom, this dedication of her soul completely to
God. In her biography, Syncletica is compared to the
famous virgin and martyr St. Thecla, who was reputed
to have been a disciple of St. Paul. Thecla had committed herself to perpetual virginity after hearing St. Paul
preach about the importance of consecrating oneself to
Christ. Her biographer said of St. Syncletica, "I think
Thecla's sufferings were milder, for the evil of the enemy

was diminished since he attacked her from outside. But in Syncletica's case, he demonstrates his more piercing brand of evil by disturbing her from within, through her own contrary and destructive thoughts."[13]

Syncletica didn't suffer physically, she wasn't attacked as a martyr, but she did struggle in this case. She had to deal with the fact that as a young woman, marriage was a viable option for her, and her parents were displeased by her choice. Also, she had natural desires to be a wife and a mother, and she had to willingly sacrifice all of these things in order to give herself to Jesus. However, she would not be persuaded by her parents pleading nor by offers of wealth or gifts of jewelry or any other thing that her suitors tried to use to persuade her. She firmly said no and stayed convinced of the commitment that she had made.

In her parents' house, Syncletica began a very strict, ascetical life, using fasting as a safeguard and a foundation for the virtues that she was trying to acquire. Her parents were not sure that they understood what she was trying to do in this ascetical life and prevailed on her to give up the idea of fasting, particularly when guests were present. However, when she was made to eat more than she was used to, more than just a little bit, she became ill. And when she fasted, not only didn't she get sick like her parents were worried she would but she looked exceptionally well. She was in better health while fasting than while eating like everyone else.

---

[13]   Pseudo-Athanasius, *The Life and Regimen of the Holy and Blessed Teacher Syncletica*, 8.

Eventually her parents passed away, leaving Syncletica to take care of her sister and the family home. Like St. Anthony before her, Syncletica sold their family's property and distributed it to the poor. Taking her sister with her, she moved to the outskirts of the city and found the family tomb. They lived there for a while, separated from the world, and for several months, she prayed earnestly to understand God's will for her.

Eventually, she sent for a priest from the village to come to her. She explained to him that she had been praying and that she felt called to leave the world completely to dedicate herself more completely to solitude and to prayer. The priest wasn't sure that this was what God wanted for a woman so young, so beautiful, and all alone in the world. But Syncletica was sure, even though it was an uncommon choice in those days. In the priest's presence, she made a very important and very deliberate sign. She cut off all of her hair, the thing that was her worldly beauty, and laid it aside. This was to be a sign for her of laying aside worldly glory, a sign to him and to all the world that her soul was unadorned and pure.

And having done this, she began to live a solitary life. She made sure that her sister was well taken care of, and moved to the desert. Again, the parallels between her life and the life of St. Anthony are many. It would not be long before many people found out about her way of life and came to join her there. Over the course of our next few chapters, we'll learn about the wisdom that St. Syncletica was able to acquire during her time in the desert and the way that she shared that wisdom with those who came to dwell with her there.

CHAPTER ELEVEN

St. Syncletica's Advice for Beginners

After St. Syncletica cut her hair and received the blessing of the priest from her village, she went out into the desert. Her biographer tells us that "she kept careful watch over the first impulses of her soul, not allowing them to be led astray by physical passions. . . . Through fasting and prayer, she trimmed the thorny offshoots of her thought and if any of these managed to grow a little, she applied various kinds of penances and all sorts of austerities."[1] Right from the very beginning, Syncletica practiced vigilance, making sure that she was alert to the ways that the enemy would try to trip her up. She knew that she would not be strong enough to take on this battle alone, and so she was constantly calling on the Lord for help. She was indeed very strong, but she knew that her strength came from God.

Pseudo-Athanasius relates, "When the Enemy's campaign was being directed against her, first of all through prayer, she used to call upon her Master to join in the

---

[1]   *Life of Syncletica*, 17.

battle, for she was not strong enough to quell the onslaught of the lion by asceticism alone. And at the instant of her supplication, the Lord was at her side and the Enemy was in flight. But often too her foe would linger for battle, and the Lord would not warn off the Fiend, by this very means intending to increase the training of her virtuous soul."[2] Here we see another parallel with the life of St. Anthony, as the Lord Jesus sometimes allowed St. Syncletica to fight the devil on her own in order to develop through training an inner strength and insight into how the devil would tempt her and fight in her life. Her biographer concludes, "At this increase of gifts, she was empowered all the more for victory against the foe."[3]

Syncletica's ascetical life included taking very rough bread in small amounts, often taking no water at all and then only when necessary, sleeping always on the bare ground, and being constant in her prayer. She was known for practicing all the virtues, especially faith, hope, and love, and giving alms on any occasion that she could. Being separated from the world and living in the desert, she wasn't always able to give alms directly, but she had a generous spirit, which was seen most often in the way that she welcomed those who came out to see her. Her reputation spread fairly quickly, and although she continued to live apart, women from the city began to hear about her way of life.

When women came to see her, the first question that they asked her was, "How should we be living in order to

---

2   Ibid., 18.
3   Ibid.

be saved?" This same kind of question we hear in the Gospels as people come out to see John the Baptist in the desert. Her visitors would beg Syncletica to speak to them, although she would tell them over and over again that she was just a beginner herself, who hadn't yet learned what she ought to know about serving the Lord. "She said to them, 'Why do you hold this fantasy about a sinner like me, as if I were doing or saying something worthwhile? We have a common teacher, the Lord, and we draw water from the same well, the Old and New Testaments.' But they would say to her, 'What you have received as a gift, give as a gift' (Mt 10:8)."[4]

Syncletica lived in the desert until her late sixties, when she developed a serious illness. As her biographer says, "The Devil, who hates good, was shriveling up, since he was unable to tolerate such an abundance of goodness. He kept trying to devise a scenario in his mind whereby he could thwart the progress of her virtues. Finally he challenged that most noble virgin to the ultimate contest."[5] Syncletica developed cancer in her lungs, and then a flu afflicted her for three and a half years that gave her a fever, burned her insides, and made it difficult for her to breathe. After this came a degenerative infection in a tooth, which quickly destroyed her jaw and her tongue.

Perhaps we can perceive the hidden plan behind this particular debilitating disease. By attacking her mouth, the devil attacked her gift of speech, through which she had taught so many people. This was the way that she had

---

4   Ibid., 21.

5   Ibid., 104.

served the Lord and her neighbor, and now this particular illness was silencing her. Through it all, she became a model of patience for those around her, and taught patience to those who came to tend to her in her illness. Her tumors were very foul-smelling, so they asked her to use perfumed ointments that would give her relief. She was reluctant to do this so that she would be able to offer her sufferings to the Lord and, in turn, encourage those people around her to have to be patient as they came and tended to her.

Syncletica suffered from these terrible pains in her jaw for more than three months. Eventually she knew that the end was near, and through writing, she indicated to her sisters that in three days more she would die. She died on the day she had predicted, at the age of eighty.

Of the 113 chapters of the *Life of Saint Syncletica*, 80 chapters—70 percent of the whole book—relate a discourse that she delivered on the spiritual life. (Again, the parallel to the *Life of Saint Anthony* is obvious.) The discourse includes much practical spiritual advice, especially as it relates to those who are beginning the kind of life that she had been living in the desert. First of all, she stressed the importance of discerning clearly the Lord's call. She begins, "I am telling you these things to safeguard you from the Adversary. What is being said, however, is not suitable for all, but only for those who choose this life. Just as one diet is not suitable for all animals, so the same instruction is not appropriate for all people."[6] Syncletica was very patient with the fact that people were coming to

---

6   Ibid., 43.

her for various reasons, but she wanted to make sure that they knew why they were there. It's wise advice for us as well, as we try to learn from her wisdom and her example, to understand why we are listening and to understand whether what she's saying applies to us and how.

"Those who find satisfaction in contemplation and spiritual enlightenment are nourished in one way," Syncletica teaches, "while those who have a taste for asceticism and its practical application are nourished in another way, and similarly those in the world who practice good works to the best of their ability."[7] This teaching of St. Syncletica, which seems very obvious to us today, is that everyone serves the Lord in the place that God knows best for them. God has a plan for each person that is specific to that person.

Next, Syncletica notes that we must be aware of the things that arise in our hearts as they are coming up, and if sins and temptations come up in us, we have to be on our guard to put a stop to them right at the right moment. But the way that beginners handle this must be suited to their condition. "It is necessary to put a stop to the beginnings of vanity at the right moment, but also again to give praise and to express admiration."[8] Here we see the complementarity of the sexes at work. While the Desert Fathers could be very matter-of-fact, sometimes harshly so, with beginners, Syncletica takes a different, motherly, approach. "If a soul does some small good," she insists, "one should admire and flatter it." On the other hand, "Its serious and

---

[7]   Ibid.

[8]   Ibid., 52.

inhuman faults should be spoken of as very slight and of no account."[9] The true amma knows how to encourage and support the beginner to make further progress. "For in the case of newly-converted and less firmly committed souls, the Devil places all their sins before their eyes" in order to discourage them. Thus, it is the responsibility of those who are helping others to make a new beginning, not to make them afraid and not to correct them too harshly. "Souls, then, that have been thus shaken should be comforted."[10]

"For those who are making their way to God, there is at first great struggle and effort, but then indescribable joy," Syncletica explains.[11] A beautiful and intriguing parable illuminates this point. When one is trying to light a fire, she explains, it happens in stages. "For just as those who wish to kindle a fire are at first choked with smoke, suffer watery eyes, and in this way achieve their purpose (indeed Scripture says, *Our God is a consuming fire*), so we too must kindle the divine fire within us with tears and effort."[12] When you first light a fire, the first thing that you get is not flames, but smoke. The important thing at this stage is perseverance, a willingness to endure the initial suffering that comes with detachment from the world. "Some, too, through their remissness, have endured the smoke, but have not kindled the fire because they did not have the perseverance and, even more, because their

---

9   Ibid.

10   Ibid.

11   Ibid., 60.

12   Ibid.

attachment to the Divine was tenuous and uncertain."[13]
God is the blazing fire of love, and our goal is to allow his
love to become like that flame in us, but we have to endure
the smoke along the way as our impurities are burned out
of us.

Syncletica uses another poignant image to describe
the beginnings of conversion, one that seems to have no
parallel in any of the other Desert Fathers or Mothers.
Recall her initial step toward the desert: in the presence
of the priest, she cut off all of her hair. This seems to have
become a first step for the women who joined her in the
desert, because she uses this to illustrate the kind of commitment to conversion that is required of them, speaking of
it as something with which they would all be familiar. She
says to her sisters, "We ought not to make our treatment of
the soul superficial, but we ought to put our soul in order
throughout, paying particular attention to its depths." "We
have cut our hair off," she says. "At the same time, let
us remove also the 'lice' on our heads."[14] She continues,
"Our 'hair', you see, was the worldly element in life: hon-
ors, fame, possession of goods, splendid outfits. . . . These
we thought it wise to discard. But rather let us cast off
the soul-devouring 'lice', some of which are these: slander, perjury, avarice."[15] Now that they have given up the
big things, and detached themselves from the world, they
must not forget about the little things, the things that are
not really so little after all because of the impact they have

---

[13]   Ibid.

[14]   Ibid., 80.

[15]   Ibid.

on the soul. "Our 'head', then, is the soul. As long as the 'lice' were sheltered in the 'hair' of worldly affairs, they seem to escape notice. But now, stripped of cover, they are visible to all. In a nun or a monk, even the minor sins are conspicuous."[16]

This is the challenge for us as well, to find in our daily routines some quiet place in our hearts. We need enough solitude and separation from whatever obstacles keep us from God to take a really good look at these subtle internal things, these little "lice" on the scalp of our soul, and to pick them off and to root them out. This is a work that continues throughout our lives.

This task requires commitment and perseverance, honesty with oneself and a willingness to look closely at the state of one's soul. Syncletica counsels her sisters always to be vigilant in this regard. "We should not be careless," she says, "but should maintain our vigilance. For the more athletes make progress, the more they are matched with stronger opponents." She goes on, "Consider how much you have advanced, and you will not underestimate the present situation."[17] Recall that this word, *athlete*, means a wrestler, someone who develops strength at hand-to-hand combat. Syncletica describes herself and her sisters as athletes who develop their strength over time, precisely by engaging in combat with the devil and with the unconverted self. We ought not be afraid to develop strength in this way, nor be surprised if the more that we grow in the spiritual life, the worse our struggles with temptations

---

[16]   Ibid.
[17]   Ibid., 26.

become for a while. Syncletica's battle went on throughout her entire life. Through it, she acquired experience and wisdom, and had advice not just for beginners but for those who are well advanced in the spiritual life.

Chapter Twelve

St. Syncletica's Wisdom
for Life's Journey

O ver long years in the desert, St. Syncletica appreciated how much it took to stay there and to persevere.
And she shared with the sisters who came to live with
her the importance of developing spiritual endurance. She
said to them, "Do not bolt when the enemy checks you,
for he himself is confounded by your steadfastness."[1] In
other words, the very willingness of the sisters to be in the
desert, and simply to stay where they were, would send
the devil away. He was trying to get them to run away
themselves, and the fact that they were willing to just
tough it out would give him pause. She goes on, "Those
who are beginning a sea voyage first encounter a favoring
wind when they have unfurled their sails. But later, a contrary wind blows against them. The sailors, however, do
not dock the ship waiting for a fortuitous breeze, but they

---

[1] *Life of Syncletica*, 102.

continue their voyage after lying quiet for a little while, or even having battled against the storm blast. So we too shall complete our voyage successfully when we encounter an opposing wind, if we raise the Cross in place of the sail."[2]

Many Desert Fathers used the cross, where the Lord Jesus was fixed with nails, as a model of endurance. But the particular image that she uses here, picturing the cross as the main mast of the ship tossed by the sea, gives a special glimpse into the life of this saint. Although she is best known for the decades that she spent in the desert, the images she uses most often in her spiritual advice are connected to the sea, and particularly to building and sailing ships. In fact, six of the twenty-seven sayings attributed to Syncletica in the *Alphabetikon*—20 percent of the total—have to do with ships. Remember that she grew up in Alexandria, an important port city and the home of the *Pharos*, the large lighthouse that was one of the Seven Wonders of the ancient world. Perhaps in her childhood her father or another relative or friend would take her for walks along the sea, where she could observe the ships coming in and out of port, watch the sailors loading and unloading their vessels, and hear the tales of their voyages. Whatever the explanation, Syncletica uses images of the sea and ships quite often, in places where we would expect different, land-based, analogies. When Syncletica speaks about vigilance, for example, she puts it this way:

---

[2]   Ibid.

Our mind must become painstakingly diligent with respect to its thoughts. We are sailing in uncertainty. For our life is a sea. . . . But some parts of the sea are full of reefs, and some full also of monsters, but some, too, are calm. We seem to be sailing in the calm, . . . during the day. It often happens, however, that the secular person has saved his ship in the midst of storm and darkness by crying out and staying awake. We, on the other hand, have drowned in calm waters, through carelessness and letting go of the rudder of righteousness. Let the one standing firm, therefore, take care lest he fall.[3]

Again, in regard to purity of heart, "Like a ship, our soul is sometimes engulfed by the waves without, and is sometimes swamped by the bilge-water within. We must guard against onslaughts of spirits from outside us, and bail out the impurities of thoughts inside us. Against the storm waves outside, salvation often comes from ships nearby, when the sailors cry out for help. But bilge waters overflow, and frequently kill the sailors, often when they are asleep and the sea is calm."[4]

Her biographer seems to have been drawn in by this tendency and also uses an example from shipping and shipbuilding to describe Syncletica's ascetical life. "She would take care of her body when her ship, so to speak, was in calm waters. Those who sail ships go without food when stormy weather and high seas overtake them, . . . but

---

3   Ibid., 47–48.

4   Ibid., 45.

when they succeed in recovering, then they take thought for a second kind of salvation. They welcome the briefest calm spell as rest from their labors. But even so they neither pass their time free from care, nor sink into deep sleep . . . since, with experience of the past, they take thought for the future. Even if the storm has abated, still, what caused it is at hand."[5]

Speaking of the importance of desiring a more intimate communion with God, through detachment, Syncletica says that "those who have endured the labors and dangers of the sea, and then amass material riches, even when they have gained much, desire to gain yet more. They consider what they have at present as nothing, and reach out for what they have not got. We, who have nothing of that which we desire, wish to acquire everything through the fear of God."[6] She was hoping that her sisters would always desire to grow in holiness, that even though they had made such a great decision by leaving the city and coming to the desert, they would see it only as a beginning.

Progress, she insists, comes only from a complete trust in God, and a distrust of the changing movements of the heart. "Just as a ship sailing without rudders is constantly tossed about," she warns, "so danger is ever gusting against negligent souls. They are not able to reach a safe harbor, since they have dropped the Lord as their pilot."[7] At the heart of her spiritual teaching, then, is a humble trust in the Lord's providence and in the gift of divine

---

5   Ibid., 19.
6   Ibid., 10.
7   Ibid., 85.

grace. "Just as one cannot build a ship unless one has some nails," she says, "so it is impossible to be saved without humility."[8] This simple teaching is a commonplace of the spiritual life, and many spiritual writers, beginning with the Lord himself (e.g., Mt 7:24–27), have explained it in terms of building a house on a solid foundation. Yet she again returns to her favorite topic of ships and shipbuilding. Perhaps amid all of this hard-won wisdom, Syncletica is subtly teaching yet another important part of the spiritual life: that God takes each of his sons and daughters where they are and incorporates their personal histories, personalities, talents, and interests into his plan for their spiritual growth and flourishing. A full explanation will have to wait for the life of heaven, but Syncletica's quirky references to the sea remind us how, in our pursuit of holiness, "in everything God works for good with those who love him, who are called according to his purpose" (Rom 8:28).

In order to persevere in the spiritual life, Syncletica was very anxious that her sisters show mercy and forgive past offenses, lest they preoccupy the mind and heart. "It is essential," she says, "to be on guard against remembrance of many wrongs, for many terrible consequences develop from it: envy, sadness, and malicious talk. The evil of these vices is lethal, even if they seem to occur in small doses."[9] Like St. Anthony, she sees that divisions and bitterness in a community are the devil's point of entry into the heart of each individual. "For these are,

---

8   *Alphabetikon*, Syncletica, 26.

9   *Life of Syncletica*, 65.

so to speak, the light weaponry of the Enemy. Often, the wounds from the two-edged blade and the larger sword (such as impurity, greed, and murder) have been healed by the medicine of conversion. Pride, however, remembrance of wrongs or malicious talk (which seem to be small weapons) have wrought destruction unnoticed, once they have been implanted into the more vital parts of the soul."[10] Such seemingly small faults poison relationships and make community life more difficult, whether in the monastery, the workplace, or the family.

Like the desert monks, Syncletica prioritized efforts at interior conversion over outward penances. "As long as we are in the monastery," she said, "obedience is preferable to asceticism. The one teaches pride, the other, humility."[11] Such penances were a means to the goal of gaining humility, but if they were taken on for the sake of impressing others, or of having one's own way, they could do great damage. Better, she says, only to take on penances with the permission of one's spiritual father or mother. "We must not seek our own will, nor follow our personal opinion, but obey our fathers in the faith."[12] Moreover, penances should be done in moderation. "A sharp knife is easily broken by a stone," after all, "and a rigid discipline soon dissolves under the influence of pride. It is appropriate, then, for the keenest discipline to take refuge in shady spots, when scorched by the heat of pride."[13]

---

[10] Ibid.

[11] Ibid., 16.

[12] Ibid., 17.

[13] Ibid., 54.

Syncletica suggests that this road of asceticism that leads to purity of heart is only possible if we are truly detached from the things of the world. She says, "Whatever we do or gain in this world, let us consider it insignificant in comparison with the eternal wealth that is to come. In the present world, we are impoverished in comparison with the Kingdom of Heaven. We have sampled the nourishment here. Let us reach for the divine! Let us live prudently in this world, so that we may obtain eternal life."[14] She counsels her sisters to accept poverty voluntarily as a safeguard against committing sins. We have noted that the story of her childhood, and her name itself, point to a wealthy, privileged upbringing, so we should not take her insistence on poverty lightly. Syncletica learned from long experience how beneficial it was for her to have left those things behind, and how her complete attachment to the Lord, though painful at first, led to true peace and fulfillment.

"The Cross is for us a trophy of victory. For our calling is nothing other than a renunciation of life, and a rehearsal of death. . . . We live by the soul. By it, let us demonstrate our virtues."[15] And so her spiritual discourse ends as it began: with a confident assurance that every sacrifice is worthwhile, every suffering meaningful, if by means of them we arrive at the goal that God has set for us—uninterrupted communion with him. Syncletica's approach, so idiosyncratic in some ways, so maternal and so patient, may seem quite a contrast to some of the Desert Fathers

---

14   Ibid., 90.
15   Ibid., 76.

we have been considering in earlier chapters. But all of them went to the desert for the same reason: to give themselves completely to the Lord, to purify their hearts and their minds so as to belong completely to him. By showing us their particular paths to holiness, they encourage us to persevere along the paths of our own lives. The last saints of the desert that we will discuss will help us to remember that this perseverance is possible even when we have stepped off the path for a while, if we can heed the Lord's call to conversion and repentance.

Part Five

Finding Healing in the Desert

CHAPTER THIRTEEN

St. Mary of Egypt: Into the Desert

When we considered the life of St. Anthony of Egypt, we saw how hearing Anthony's story led St. Augustine to the moment of crisis that marked his conversion. In turn, Augustine's conversion spread throughout the Catholic Church and continues to have an impact in our own day. Roughly contemporary with St. Augustine, two great figures of the desert also experienced powerful conversions, and their stories made as much of an impact in the Christian East as Augustine's story did in the West.

The first of these figures is known as St. Mary of Egypt, whose story is related by St. Sophronius. The story begins, however, with a desert monk known as Abba Zosimas. Born in the early fourth century in Palestine, near Caesarea, Zosimas began living in a monastery there when he was still a small child. He was very devoted to God from his earliest years, and his contemporaries testify that he became an expert in every kind of abstinence and asceticism, observing the Rule without blame. He experienced deep prayer that included mystical visions and the gift of prophecy and received frequent messages from God for his fellow monks and for those who would visit the monastery seeking prayers and miraculous healings. He became a priest in order to be able to provide the sacraments for his fellow monks, and he was often visited by people from Caesarea and the surrounding countryside.

Zosimas lived in this monastery until the age of fifty-three, and he was tempted at one point to think that he was perfect. As he writes, he began to say to himself, "Is there a monk on Earth capable of affording me benefit, or passing onto me anything new, some kind of spiritual achievement of which I either do not know or in which I have not succeeded as a monk? Surely, there can be found among the men of the desert one surpassing me in his deeds."[1] In response to his thoughts, he had a vision in which "someone stood before him and said, 'Zosimas, you have done as well as any man can. You have done well in the whole monastic way. But among human beings, no one can attain perfection. A greater ordeal lies ahead of you, although you do not know this. And so that you may know how many and varied are the ways to salvation, leave your native land . . . and go to the monastery which lies near the river Jordan.'"[2]

At this instruction, Zosimas immediately left his monastery and followed the Jordan River to a monastery near

---

[1]   Sophronius, *The Life of Saint Mary of Egypt*, trans. Benedicta Ward in *Harlots of the Desert: A Study of Repentance in Early Monastic Sources* (Kalamazoo, Mich.: Cistercian Pub., 1987), 2.

[2]   Ibid.

Jerusalem, about ninety miles to the south. When he arrived, he would not give his name and was accepted there as a stranger rather than the famous monk he had become in Caesarea. Immediately, he was put to work in the lowest place among the monks, and he accepted this as if he were a beginner in the monastic life. He was immediately impressed by the example of the old men who lived there, saying that "every one burned with the love of God." They were all completely detached from their possessions and served one another with great love. Zosimas realized that perhaps he was wrong about how far he had advanced and that in fact he had a great deal farther to go in the way of perfection.

The monks of that monastery had a custom for observing the period of Lent in preparation for the Easter feasts. On the first Sunday of Lent, after gathering for Mass and receiving Holy Communion, each one of them took a little bit of food for the journey and left the monastery. A few of them stayed behind to tend to the needs of the sick and to pray for the rest who were going out, but most of them walked out together as far as the Jordan. Crossing over, they separated, each going his own way to seek a quiet place in the wilderness to spend the weeks of the Great Fast. Most would have spent the time in solitude; a few perhaps would encounter a hermit living there from whom they would receive advice. On Palm Sunday, they would return to the monastery, each keeping the story of his Lenten retreat to himself.

In 452, Zosimas went out as usual with the other monks. That year, he walked through the desert continually, stopping only for food or sleep when nature commanded him to. He slept on the ground, but he felt a great urgency to keep moving, to keep going deeper and deeper into the desert, in hopes of finding someone there who could guide him and help him in a particular spiritual struggle. He recounts feeling a tug in his heart, like he was hastening along to a well-known inn, some place that he was expected, although he had never been there before. He felt that God was leading him, but he wasn't sure exactly where it was that he was supposed to be going.

Zosimas walked for three weeks, and on the twenty-first day of his journey, he stopped at noon and knelt down to pray. When he was finished his prayers, he opened his eyes, and before he stood up, he noticed that there was a shadow next to him on the ground. He was afraid and made the Sign of the Cross, thinking that it might be some wild animal or evil spirit casting the shadow. When the shadow didn't move, he felt that it was something safe. He turned around and saw a person standing next to him, a human being with very long hair and very darkened skin that had been tanned by the sun. As soon as he turned around, the figure ran away from him, so he chased after it.

As he drew close, the person jumped into a bush. He called after the person to come out, and he heard something quite unexpected: the voice of a woman. She refused to come out until he threw his cloak in after her, because she had no clothes. When she emerged, she asked him, "Zosimas, why are you here?" He had never laid eyes on her before, nor been in that part of the desert, and so

Zosimas was mystified at being called by name by this stranger. Impressed by her obvious austerity of life and her apparently mystical knowledge, Zosimas knelt and asked for her blessing. The woman also knelt, insisting that, as a priest, it was more proper for Zosimas to impart a blessing to her—again demonstrating a mystical gift of knowledge. After arguing for a time over who had the right to bless the other, they prayed together for a while and then stood.

Zosimas earnestly desired to know more about his new acquaintance, convinced already of her holiness. "O Mother in the Spirit," he said, "it is plain that all your life, you have dwelt with God, and have nearly died to the world. It is plain, above all, that grace is given you, since you called me by my name and recognized me as a priest, although you have never seen me before."[3] Her response surprised him: "Blessed be God who cares for the salvation of souls," she began. "Be assured, sir, that I am just a woman and a sinner, but protected by holy Baptism. God deliver us, Father Zosimas, from the Enemy and his emissaries, for his envy of us is great."[4]

Zosimas pleaded with the woman to tell him her story, but she hesitated, insisting that she was nothing, no one worth talking about, and that he ought to turn around and go back where he came from. After much pleading, Zosimas convinced her, and she told him that her name was Mary and that she was born in Alexandria around the year 376. Her home, she said, was a happy one. Her family was

---

[3]   Ibid., 10.

[4]   Ibid., 10–11.

Christian. There was nothing in her home life to cause any problems, nothing for her to complain about in the way that she was brought up. We should keep in mind that Alexandria was the provincial capital of Egypt and a prominent city, a center of learning and commerce, a crossroads and an important port.

From Mary's own account, she was much taken by the life of this metropolis. She left home, she says, at the age of twelve and lost her virginity soon after that. At that point, she was very frank about what happened to her. She realized, she said, how much she enjoyed the sexual relationships that she entered into and gave herself over to a life of promiscuity for seventeen years. She says it was not for any desire to profit from it—she was not a prostitute—but simply out of insatiable desire. In fact, she lived a very impoverished life, making what little money she had by begging or by spinning thread. With painful frankness, she admitted that "I wanted to wallow in this trough and that to me was life. I thought any kind of desecration to be natural."[5] For seventeen years, until she was twenty-nine, she pursued a life marked by promiscuity and lust.

A moment that would mark her lowest ebb also became the turning point in her story. One day she saw a large group of people from Egypt, Libya, and the surrounding provinces heading to the port of Alexandria. Asking one of them what was happening, she learned that these were pilgrims setting out for Jerusalem. Constantine had built a church there, over the sites of Calvary and the Holy Sepulcher, with a shrine to the holy cross, and it was arranged

---

5   Ibid., 13.

that the cross of the Lord would be exposed in a solemn liturgy.

Although she was aware of the sacred purpose of the pilgrimage, Mary experienced a desire to go along for a very different reason. She was told that anyone could go who could pay the fare, and she said to her interlocutor, "I have a body, and that will serve as food and fare for me." She admits to Zosimas that "I wanted to go (forgive me, father) so that I might soon have more lovers for my lust."[6] At the dock, she began to flirt with about a dozen young men she met there and promised that if they got her onto the boat, she would give them whatever they wanted. They agreed, and she was as good as her word. On the boat, she told Zosimas, she freely gave herself to them, to the various men on the crew, and to anyone who was interested. She even seduced, she said, people who were initially unwilling. "I am amazed, my father," she said to Zosimas, "that the sea carried my lusts and that the earth did not open to take me alive down into hell. But I think my God was seeking my repentance, for he does not desire the death of sinners but guards them in his loving kindness, waiting for them to be converted."

The pilgrimage arrived in Jerusalem, and while waiting for the festival to begin, Mary continued to seduce many men, both inhabitants of the city and pilgrims. On the day that the people gathered to see the relics of the cross exposed, perhaps September 14, she saw a large crowd going to the church of the Holy Sepulcher. More out of curiosity than for any other reason, she went along with the

---

6   Ibid.

crowd to the doors of the church. As soon as she reached the threshold where others were entering the church, she tried to enter herself. As she described it, she walked up to the archway and tried to enter and was immediately pushed back by an invisible force. She said it was as if a group of soldiers, with their shields in front of them, had thrown her back from the door.

Thinking at first that it must have been someone in front of her whom she had not noticed, she got up and tried again. Once again, she was repelled and left standing in the courtyard. Three or four more times, she tried in vain to enter the church, and finally was worn out. By this time, everyone had entered the church, and Mary was left alone in the portico. She said, "Only then did I begin to see why it was that I was prevented from going in to see the life-giving wood [of the cross]. For a salutary understanding touched my mind and the eyes of my heart, and showed me that it was the sinfulness of my actions that prevented me from going in. So I began to weep and grieve and beat my breast; I drew sighs and tears from the bottom of my heart."[7]

We see here the extraordinary power of God to draw a soul to himself. For seventeen years, Mary had been doing exactly what she wanted. For seventeen years, she had not been listening to God, nor to her own conscience, but had been pushing that voice away, closing her ears to anything except her desires and temptations. Now, in an instant, God's voice broke through, and gave her light.

She noticed on the wall of the courtyard an icon of the

---

[7]   Ibid., 16.

Virgin Mary. As Mary of Egypt says, gazing directly into the eyes of that icon, she began to pray:

> Virgin and Lady, who gave birth to the Word of God according to the flesh, I see now that it is not suitable and decent for me, defiled as I am, to look upon this picture of you . . . who always kept your body and soul chaste and clean from all sin. Indeed, it would be right for you in your purity to reject and loathe my impurity. But God, to whom you gave birth, became man, as I have heard, to save sinners and to call them to repentance. So help me, for I am alone and without any other help.[8]

Confident that, as St. Paul says, "The saying is sure and worthy of full acceptance, that Christ Jesus came into the world to save sinners" (1 Tm 1:15), Mary continued her prayer for Our Lady's intercession and for God's mercy.

> Receive my confession and give me leave to enter the church. Do not deprive me of the sight of that most precious wood upon which was fixed God made man, whom you carried and bore as a Virgin, and where he gave his blood for my redemption. O Lady, let the doors be opened to me so that I may adore the divine Cross. I beg you, from whom Christ took flesh, to guarantee my promise, which is that I will never again defile my flesh by immersing it in horrifying lusts. As soon as I have seen the Cross of

---

[8]   Ibid.

your Son, holy Virgin, I will go wherever you as my
mediator for salvation shall order and lead.[9]

Mary tried once more to enter the church, and this time
she is able to walk through the door. She went into the
sanctuary with the other pilgrims who had gathered there
and arrived just as the Patriarch was holding up the cross
for the veneration of the faithful. Realizing in that moment
how God hears the prayers of the repentant, she knelt and
kissed the dust of the floor, and then left the church full
of joy. The life of St. Mary of Egypt does not explicitly
mention her receiving sacramental confession, but we see
from this story that she was certainly reconciled in these
moments. She certainly experienced the forgiving and
absolving love of the Lord, and she left the church with
her sins forgiven, reconciled to God.

On her way out, she returned to the icon of the Blessed
Virgin Mary. Giving thanks profusely, she remembered
the promise she made. "It is time, Lady, to keep the pledge
which I made with you as my witness and to fulfill that
which I promised. Now, therefore, lead me wherever
you please; lead me to salvation, teach me what is true,
and go before me in the way of repentance."[10] At once,
Mary heared a voice far off, saying, "If you cross the Jordan, you will find a place to rest." Taking this as a sign
from heaven, she determined to follow it. But she was a
stranger in Jerusalem, so she needed to ask for directions
to find the Jordan River. As she set out, a stranger walked

---

9   Ibid.
10   Ibid., 17.

up to her in the crowd and said, "Mother, take this," handing her three coins. With them, she bought three loaves of bread and then left the next morning at 9:00. At sunset, she reached the church of St. John the Baptist at the Jordan and received the Eucharist. She ate half of one of those loaves of bread and slept on the ground that night, and the next day, she crossed the Jordan River. Her journey into the desert, which became her journey of repentance and conversion, would last the next forty-seven years.

CHAPTER FOURTEEN

Desert Conversions: St. Mary of Egypt and St. Moses the Ethiopian

St. Mary of Egypt

When Mary crossed over the Jordan, she went continually deeper into the desert. She related to Abba Zosimas that, of the forty-seven years she spent in the desert, the first seventeen were full of terrible temptations. Lust, hunger, and memories of her early life distracted and oppressed her. Of course, she saw these as reparation for the seventeen years she had spent in promiscuity and lust, and so she was able to face these challenges with resignation and patience. By the end of this time, her supply of bread had long run out, but God gave her the ability to survive on the herbs and grasses she could find growing in the wilderness. Her clothing soon wore out and fell apart, and she was left to cover her nakedness with her long hair.

Mary relates that during this trying time, when memories of her former way of life came back to her, she strove to recall the memory of the day of her conversion. "In my mind," she says, "I would come before the picture of the holy Mother of God, who had accepted me on trust, and implore her to chase from me those thoughts which were afflicting my most wretched soul. I would fling myself on the ground and flood the earth with weeping, hoping that she would stand by me, who had been my guarantor."[1] In other words, Mary of Egypt was well aware that she had made a promise to the Blessed Virgin, but she also felt that in that moment in the church of the Holy Sepulcher, the Virgin Mary had made a promise to her. And now that she knew that she had no strength to face this way of penance and asceticism on her own, she needed to call on that promise.

"Often," she says. "I directed the eyes of my heart to her, my guarantor, praying to her without ceasing to help me in this solitude to repentance. For I have her as my helper, whose purity bore our Creator. From that time to this," Mary relates, "my helper, the Mother of God, has been with me, and she directs me in all things."[2]

Very impressed by her story, Zosimus knelt at this point and asked for her prayers. In turn, Mary asked Zosimus for a favor. She said in all the time that she'd been in the desert, she had not seen another human being and had not received the Holy Eucharist since the day she crossed the Jordan. The following Lent, she explained, rather than go out on the first Sunday of Lent, as was the custom in his monastery, he would stay in the monastery. She insisted

---

[1]   *Life of St. Mary of Egypt*, 19.
[2]   Ibid.

that he must do this for her, saying that even if he tried, he would not be able to go out. On Holy Thursday, she said, she would meet him at the Jordan River. She wanted him to bring her the Eucharist from Mass that day so that she could receive the Lord in the Blessed Sacrament. In the meantime, she insisted, he was to tell no one that they had met, nor relate her story to any other person. It was a great struggle for him to keep her secret all year, but before he left, she insisted that he make her this promise.

The following year, Abba Zosimus did as St. Mary had asked him. On Holy Thursday—April 12, 453—he went out from his monastery to the banks of the Jordan River. Sitting there in the moonlight, he wondered how Mary was going to get across the water to him; neither of them had a boat. Finally, he saw Mary coming, and as she arrived at the bank, he saw her make the sign of the cross over the water, and then walk across the water to him as if it were solid glass.

Mary and Zosimas recited the Creed and the Our Father together, and then exchanged the kiss of peace. She received Holy Communion from him very devoutly, and then together they prayed the canticle of Simeon from the Gospel of Luke, which begins, "Lord, now let thy servant depart in peace, according to thy word" (Lk 2:29). Abba Zosimas had brought a basket of food along with him, full of dates, figs, bread, and other fruit and vegetables, hoping that she would take it with her. Smiling, Mary took only three lentils for her sustenance, telling Zosimas that "the grace of the Holy Spirit is sufficient to keep whole the substance of the soul."[3] Finally, they took their leave of each other, amid pleas from Zosimas that they should meet again the following year. Mary promised that if Zosimas returned the following Lent to the place where they originally met, he would see her again.

Zosimas kept this appointment the following year, though it took some wandering through the desert for him to find the place. Again, he felt himself led by a divine impulse, as if God was leading him back to the spot. On his arrival, he found an unexpected sight: Mary's body was lying dead on the ground. Out of concern for him, she had left him a note written in the sand. She died, the note explained, on the very night that Zosimas last saw her, after she received the Eucharist on Holy Thursday the previous year. This meant that she had made the journey that took Abba Zosimas three weeks in the matter of a few hours. In addition to that miracle is the fact that not only her body but also her writing was preserved all year— the note which explained the circumstances of her death, which she had foreseen by a divine gift, and which asked Zosimas to bury her body.

Unsure of how to proceed at his age and in such a deserted place, Zosimas found a piece of wood and began to dig a hole in the dry ground. Our familiarity with the stories of the desert should prepare us for what happened next: A lion came running through the desert and dug a grave for Mary. After Zosimas placed her body in the grave and prayed for her, the lion filled in the grave and,

---

[3]   Ibid., 22.

after seeking a blessing from Zosimas, ran off into the desert.

Now that he no longer had to keep the secret, once Zosimas returned to his monastery for Easter, the story of St. Mary of Egypt spread very rapidly throughout the area. It was first recorded by the bishop of Jerusalem, St. Sophronius, in the seventh century. To this day, the fifth Sunday of Lent is kept as St. Mary of Egypt Sunday in the Eastern Catholic and Orthodox Churches, when the story of her life is read in the church as an example and model of repentance.

Why do we tell such a story? As painful as it is in its early details, it is also a model for us of repentance and an encouragement, no matter the extent of our own sins, to open our hearts to receive God's mercy. When we encounter the depths of God's mercy in the life of a sinner like St. Mary, who was able to recount God's goodness with such frankness, generosity, and humility about her own story, it enables those who may be afraid to approach the Lord to do so with confidence. St. Paul made a similar point in his first letter to Timothy. After reminding Timothy "that Christ Jesus came into the world to save sinners," Paul goes on to admit that "I am the foremost of sinners; but I received mercy for this reason, that in me, as the foremost, Jesus Christ might display his perfect patience for an example to those who were to believe in him for eternal life" (1 Tm 1:15–16). By showering his mercy on people in extreme circumstances, like Mary of Egypt and Paul of Tarsus, and then sending them as witness to his kindness, God calls every sinner "with confidence [to] draw near to the throne of grace, that we may receive mercy and find grace to help in time of need" (Heb 4:16).

St. Moses the Ethiopian

Another famous conversion story has to do with a man who became a pillar among the Desert Fathers, and one of the most famous monks to live at the monastery at Sketis. Before he joined the monks there, however, he led a group of a different kind: a gang of thieves. He was born about the year 330 and is known as Moses the Ethiopian. He was not necessarily from the area that we now know by that name, as in the ancient world, and the Roman Empire, *Aethiopia* referred to a much larger area, most of what we call sub-Saharan Africa. The Greek word *aithiops* is derived from the Greek words for "burnt face," and was used to refer to anyone of Black African descent.

Moses was the servant of a government official in the city of Nitria, a famous mining location about sixty miles south of the capital, Alexandria. He did not hold this job for long, however, because he was dismissed for stealing from his master. He soon realized that he was good at stealing and decided to make a life of it. He gathered a gang of seventy thieves around him and turned to highway robbery, breaking and entering, and sheep rustling. On at least one occasion, he was accused of attempted murder.

When a shepherd's dog alerted a victim of one of his robberies, and Moses was nearly caught, he swore vengeance on the shepherd. He soon pursued and tracked down the shepherd, catching sight of him on the opposite bank of the Nile, which was then in flood. Moses put his knife between his teeth and, heedless of the crocodiles in the river, he crossed the Nile in pursuit of the shepherd. The shepherd ran away, so Moses took four of his best rams and slaughtered them, tied them together, and carried them on his shoulders back across the river, where he butchered the sheep, ate what he wanted, and sold the rest.

The next day, Moses was informed that the authorities were looking for him, and so he fled into the Egyptian desert. It's not clear just when his conversion happened, but at a certain point, wandering in the desert, he stumbled upon the monastery at Sketis. The monks did not ask many questions about where he had been, or what he wanted, but allowed him to stay with them for a time. He finally decided to remain there and make a home with them, and he became a disciple of Abba Isidore, one of the leading members of the community at Sketis. Later, Moses would become a disciple of Abba Macarius, who himself had been a disciple of Abba Anthony the Great at the Outer Mountain.

Moses took up life in one of the cells of the *laura* at Sketis. During his first six years in the monastery, Moses felt compelled to do very hard penance because he was still facing many temptations, mostly triggered by memories of his life before the monastery. His old habits were hard to break, and he supposed that the best way to overcome them was to occupy his time, his mind, and his body with as much asceticism as he could muster. He stood in his cell all night in prayer, and as he said, for the first six years of his time in Sketis, he never slept at night if he could help it. When he could not just stand and pray, he filled his nights with charitable works for the older monks. For example, the source of water at Sketis was five miles away from where the monks lived, and Moses would often go out in secret to fill the water jars of the elderly monks who could not make the journey themselves. One night, while out on this task, Moses relates that he was attacked by demons who beat him, so much that he became seriously ill. Someone found him there by the water and brought him back, but even after convalescing for almost a year, he never completely recovered from this assault.

Moses learned to live on just ten ounces of bread a day and fasted very strictly. He said fifty psalms throughout the course of the day to make sure that his mind was always fixed on God. Abba Isidore tried to temper Moses's ascetical practices, insisting that he "practice moderation, even the works of ascetic life," but Moses resisted. If he just fought hard enough, he believed, he could get his temptations out of the way. One morning, Isidore appeared at Moses's cell very early before dawn. He took him up a hill, and together they watched the sun come up. Isidore explained that just as the sun's rays appear little by little, and the sky brightens gradually, so in a person's spiritual life, virtue grows gradually, by degrees. Rather than try to accomplish everything at once, Isidore explained, the monk must acquire holiness through perseverance and daily struggle.

Moses struggled for a long time, especially against temptations to lust. One time, he came to Abba Isidore, overcome by passions, overcome by temptations to lust. "The old man exhorted him to return to his cell. But he refused, saying, 'Abba, I cannot.' Then Abba Isidore took Moses out onto the terrace and said to him, 'Look towards the west.' He looked, and saw hordes of demons flying about and making a noise before launching an attack. Then Abba Isidore said to him, 'Look toward the east.' He turned and saw an innumerable multitude of heavenly angels shining with glory. Abba Isidore said, 'See, these are sent by the Lord to the saints to bring them help, while those in the west fight against them. Those who are with us are more in number than they are.' Then Abba Moses gave thanks to God, plucked up courage and returned to his cell."[4]

Notice what Abba Isidore *did not* say. He did not tell Moses that he would not have to fight, that the angels would take care of everything. Nor did he promise Moses that he would not face temptations; in fact, he showed him just how many enemies were arrayed against him. Rather, he gave him one simple reason to maintain his trust and perseverance: "Those on our side are more than those on their side." Moses would have to fight, but he would be able to count on God's strength and protection to come to his aid. With that in mind, Moses was able to go and fight a little longer.

A third time Moses came back to Abba Isidore to complain about these temptations, which had become extremely strong, such that he was beginning to despair of his vocation as a monk. Taking him to the church, Abba Isidore prayed over Moses and said to him, "In the Name of Jesus Christ, from this time forward the demons shall

---

[4]   *Alphabetikon*, Moses 1.

cease from attacking you. Come now and receive the Holy Mysteries [the Eucharist] and you will be free from all impurity of the flesh and the spirit. Do not boast within yourself and say, 'I have overcome the demons,' for it was for your benefit that they fought so against you."[5] Although Moses had tried for so long to fight these temptations on his own, in the end, Abba Isidore made it clear that only divine grace could accomplish his healing and give him real freedom. He urged Moses to be grateful for the wisdom and strength he had gained in the battle, but always to remember that the ultimate victory belonged to God alone.

---

[5] *The Life of Our Holy Father Among the Saints Moses the Ethiopian*, trans. the Monks of Holy Transfiguration Monastery (Seattle: St. Nectarios Press, 1991), p. 6.

CHAPTER FIFTEEN

St. Moses the Ethiopian: A Convert's Wisdom

St. Moses developed a great reputation in the monastery of Sketis and in the surrounding area. He had many visitors, but he was careful to maintain his humility despite the fact that people were coming to regard him as a living saint. For example, one day a high-ranking official from the local town came looking for him. He stopped at the monastery gate to ask directions to where Abba Moses's cell was and then proceeded along his way. Abba Moses lived on a bit of a hill, so he saw the man and his retinue coming from a distance and decided to head him off along the way.

When he met him on the road, the man stopped and asked, not knowing who Moses was, how to get to the old man's cave. Moses looked at him, and without introducing himself said, "What do you want with him? He is a fool." So the magistrate went back to the church and told the other monks what had happened. "When they heard this, the clergy were offended and said, 'What kind of an old man was it who spoke like that about the holy man to you?' He said, 'An old man wearing old clothes, a big black man.' They said, 'It was Abba Moses himself and it was in order not to meet you that he said that.' The magistrate went away greatly edified."[1]

The magistrate was not the only person to have an unusual encounter with Abba Moses. "One day four thieves came to the righteous one's cell to rob him of anything they might find. They did not know that he was the former infamous thief. Moses, still quite strong and powerful easily overcame them and proceeded to tie them up. He then lifted the four on his shoulders and carried them to the main church of Sketis."[2] This detail makes us recall his swim across the Nile, with the shepherd's four best rams tied up and carried on his shoulders. But his time in the desert has had such an effect on Moses that the outcome this time is much different. "He said to the fathers gathered there, 'It is not allowed for me, the penitent, to chastise these men by myself. I caught them in the act of attempted robbery and I have brought them to you. What do you command that I do with them?'"[3] The four robbers were so impressed with Moses's restraint that they immediately confessed and repented, and even stayed to become monks at Sketis and spiritual sons of Abba Moses.

In his later years, Moses was ordained a priest. He did not want to accept ordination, believing he was unworthy

---

[1]   *Alphabetikon*, Moses 8.
[2]   *Life of Moses*, p. 8.
[3]   Ibid.

of it given his past sins and present weakness. But the elders of the monastery prevailed upon him, insisting that they needed someone to celebrate the Eucharist and the other sacraments for them. Moses reluctantly accepted this new responsibility, while recommitting himself to living as humbly and as isolated as possible so as to avoid temptations to pride and vanity. He refused to be waited on by the younger monks and withdrew as much as possible from any kind of interaction that would lead people to think that he was somehow special or important.

Moses lived in the desert until he was seventy-five years old. In the last few years of his life, he moved away from Sketis to the nearby monastery of Petra, which was more isolated and where he hoped he could find more solitude, to prepare himself for death. When barbarians invaded the region around Alexandria and came to Sketis, Moses sent his disciples away, but he remained behind to give them time to escape and to offer his life as a martyr. They prevailed on him to flee, but Moses replied, "For many years I have waited for this day so that the words of our Lord might be fulfilled: 'They who live by the sword shall die by the sword.' How could I leave now and lose my crown?"[4] Seven of his disciples insisted on remaining with him, and six of them were slain with Moses. Moses died on August 28 so that he shares his feast day with his fellow penitent, St. Augustine.

Moses, who had been the head of a gang of seventy thieves during his lifetime, died leaving behind him seventy disciples. They learned above all from his humility,

---

4   Ibid., p. 13.

which was the fruit of his commitment to repentance. Moses did not make light of his sins, but he did not want to be weighed down by them either. Rather, he relied completely on God's love and mercy, and spoke openly (like St. Mary of Egypt and St. Paul) of how much he had been forgiven. This led him to be an apostle of mercy towards others, and he commanded his disciples to imitate him in being ready to forgive and to extend patience and mercy to their brothers.

One of the most important, and impressive, stories about Abba Moses deals with this theme of learning to forgive others through mindfulness of one's own sins. One day at Sketis, a brother in the community had committed a serious fault, a grave sin. A council of the elders of the monastery was called to deal with the situation. From the context, we gather that the brother was probably going to be thrown out. Moses was summoned to this assembly but refused to attend. The elders sent a messenger to Moses's cell, insisting that he attend and saying that they would not start the meeting without him.

After a while, they spotted Moses coming along the road to the gathering place, obviously weighed down by some heavy burden. As he drew closer, they saw that it was a large basket filled with sand, though they could not understand why he was carrying it. Soon they noticed that the basket had a hole in it and that a trail of sand extended behind Moses back to the area of his cell. When he arrived, the elders asked what this gesture meant. Looking first at the accused brother, and then at the assembly, he said quietly, "My many sins run out behind me, and

I do not see them, and today I am coming to judge the error of another."[5] Challenged and edified by his words, the assembly agreed to forgive the brother and give him a second chance.

Abba Moses was convinced about how important it is in a community (as in a family) not to judge another person harshly. "The monk must die to his neighbor," he insists, "and never judge him in any way. When someone is occupied with his own faults, he doesn't see those of his neighbor."[6] Because he focused his attention on his own need for mercy, Moses was able to be merciful to those around him.

Along with his deep commitment to conversion and penance, Abba Moses was also gifted with a generous and hospitable heart. Hospitality was a key virtue in the desert, as we see many times in the Scriptures and in other ancient texts. Although the desert monks took on strict fasting as a bodily penance, the general rule was relaxed when visitors came and hospitality was required. The abba who received guests ate and drank with them, and then did his penance in another way or at another time. Moses was known for being very welcoming and generous to all who came to visit him. It was a mark of his humility and of the joy that he felt in having been received so generously by the fathers when he was in need. On at least one occasion, others in the monastery were scandalized by how freely Moses received guests and ate with them, even when a special fast had been proclaimed, and they reported his

---

5   *Alphabetikon*, Moses 2.

6   Ibid., Moses 1a, 3a.

apparent transgression to the elders. In front of the young monks, the abbot questioned Moses and, satisfied that his charity and hospitality were genuine, said, "Abba Moses, you did not keep the commandment of men, but it was so that you might keep the commandment of God."[7] Just as the purpose of ascetical practices is to lead one to a deeper love of God, rather than to be an end in themselves, likewise asceticism ought to increase one's love of neighbor.

When we discussed St. Syncletica and her method of giving spiritual advice, we saw the reality that God called real, whole people to live in the desert—with their history, experience, and personality very much in evidence. Lest we think that the life of the desert was only practiced by austere, grouchy men, people like Abba Moses displayed great cheerfulness, born of an appreciation for God's goodness and a trust in his providence. The *Alphabetikon* relates a beautiful, intriguing story that is worth quoting in full:

> It was told of a brother who came to Sketis that, when he came to the church, he asked the clergy if he could visit Abba Arsenius. They said to him, "Brother, have a little refreshment and then go and see him." "I shall not eat anything," said he, "till I have met him." So, because Arsenius's cell was far away, they sent a brother with him. Having knocked on the door, they entered, greeted the old man and sat down without saying anything. Then the brother from the church said, "I will leave you. Pray for

---

7   Ibid., Moses 5.

me." Now the visiting brother, not feeling at ease with the old man, said, "I will come with you," and they went away together.

Then the visitor asked, "Take me to Abba Moses, who used to be a robber." When they arrived, the Abba welcomed them joyfully and then took leave of them with delight.

The brother who had brought the other one said to his companion, "See, I have brought you to the foreigner [i.e., Arsenius, born in Rome] and to the Egyptian [i.e., Moses], which of the two do you prefer?" "As for me," he replied, "I prefer the Egyptian."

Now, a Father who heard this prayed to God saying, "Lord, explain this matter to me: for Thy name's sake the one flees from men, and the other, for Thy name's sake, receives them with open arms." Then two large boats were shown to him on a river and he saw Abba Arsenius and the Spirit of God sailing in the one, in perfect peace, and in the other was Abba Moses with the angels of God, and they were all eating honey cakes.[8]

What the monk came to understand by the vision was that both of these ways of life—Arsenius in his silent contemplation and Moses in his cheerful charity—were pleasing to God. Just as the two ships kept pace with each other and sailed in the same direction, so the two monks were

---

8   Ibid., Arsenius 38.

equally making their way towards holiness and purity of heart.

Moses learned what it meant to be hospitable, sometimes at the expense of his own comfort. Towards the end of his life, Moses went from Sketis to Petra in search of a deeper silence and solitude. He wasn't running away from people, but he needed more time for prayer and communion with God. When he went to Petra, before he left, he was worried about whether he would be able to find water there. Not knowing Petra first hand, he did not know what provisions would be available. While he was thinking about this, he heard a voice say to him, "Go, and do not worry about anything."

So he went to Petra, and immediately, before he could get settled, visitors came to him. He used the little bit of water that he had brought from Sketis to cook lentils for them, but then it was all used up. Moses sat down with his visitors to eat and talk, but they could tell that he was preoccupied. Several times he rose and left the cell, raising his hands in prayer to God just outside the door. Finally, his visitors asked him what was happening. Just at that moment, clouds filled the sky over Petra and a driving rain began to fall, enough to fill all the cisterns in Petra as well as a little vessel Moses had placed outside the cell.

Moses explained to his visitors, "I was arguing with God, saying, 'You brought me here, and now I have no water for your servants.' That's why I was going in and out. I was going on at God until he sent us some water."[9]

---

[9]   Ibid., Moses 13.

Moses had learned from long experience that he could do nothing on his own but that God would always provide what was necessary for doing his will. Like his namesake Moses, who led the Israelites out of Egypt, Moses the Ethiopian was able to pray with great confidence, to say to God, "You made a promise. This was your plan, and you must keep your word and help me."

This ability to trust God completely is likewise behind one of the more mysterious words that comes down to us from Moses the Ethiopian. "A brother came to Sketis to visit Abba Moses and asked him for a word. The old man said to him, 'Go, sit in your cell, and your cell will teach you everything.'"[10] As a youth, Moses had called his own shots, doing exactly what he wanted. But the peace and freedom he found in the desert taught him the central importance of stillness, commitment, and surrender to the will of God. His word to the young monk, simple yet profound, can serve as a summary of his spiritual doctrine. Trusting that God has brought him to the place where he is living, the monk is able to rest in the knowledge that divine providence will take care of everything. When a soul has acquired this trust, there is no longer any need to be busy about many things, to give way to anxiety or temptation, or to fill one's mind with many plans. Instead, when the monk has created a place—the cell—where he is able to be "alone with God alone," his life is transformed by familiar daily communion with the divine, and he is

---

[10]   Ibid., Moses 6.

already on the path that leads to the ultimate fulfillment of heaven.

* * * * * * * * * *

This little book about the Desert Fathers and Mothers has introduced a wide variety of holy men and women: from diverse background, with particular and sometimes colorful histories, full of personality, wisdom, and strength. Of course, this brief survey has hardly scratched the surface of the wisdom to be found in the deserts of Egypt, not to mention the monks of Palestine and Syria, and their "descendants" in the great monastic communities in the East and the West through the centuries since. Hopefully this small sampling will whet the reader's appetite and be an encouragement and an invitation to draw more deeply from the rich legacy left by these heroes of the desert.

The advice of these experts in the spiritual life requires translation, of course, into the circumstances of modern life, as well as adaptation to the realities we face today. That much was true even in the fourth century, when John Cassian and others first shared the sayings and stories of the Egyptian desert with medieval Europe, adapting and refining them as they saw fit. Moreover, each reader needs to remember how the "words" of the abbas and ammas were already adapted to the particular circumstances of individual monks and nuns, and to pray for both divine and human assistance in understanding which parts of desert wisdom are directed to them. Nevertheless, every reader can pursue the one common theme that gave inspiration and strength to all of the Desert Fathers and Mothers: that the goal of the spiritual life, and of all of our prayers and sacrifices, is to attain that purity of heart which enables us to "see God" (Mt 5:8) and to commune with him in this life and in the life to come. Whether our course is steady or tumultuous, whether we spend it in silence or eating honey cakes, our destination is the same: eternal joy with God, in the communion of the saints of the desert and of every time and place, forever.